POWER OF KINGDOM MINDSET: VOLUME I

Short Stories of Believers who Transformed their Lives Through the Renewing of their Minds

Compiled by: Dr. J. Le'Ray

Series

#PowerOfKingdomMindset #POKM

Cover Design by Reginald Blanks
Interior Design by Grace Marie Brown & Dr. J. Le'Ray
Editing by Grace Marie Brown & Kristin Bellamy-Lloyd
Proofreading by Kristin Bellamy-Lloyd

ISBN: 978-0-9991562-4-7

VOLUME I

AMAZON #1 BEST SELLER BOOK

POWER OF KINGDOM MINDSET: VOLUME I
BEST SELLING CO-AUTHORS

POWER OF LOVE
Dr. Kelly Bullock Daugherty
Dani Keys
Toni Brown

POWER OF FORGIVENESS
Crystal M. Edwards
Alma R. Atkinson
ULanda R. Hunter

POWER OF HUMILITY
Ja'Quez D. Cruse
Nikki T. Tibbs
Alicia D. Foust

POWER OF APOLOGY
Yvonne Wilson Anderson
Towanda Wilson
Dr. J. Le'Ray

POWER OF TRUTH
Dr. Natalie Holts Davis
Erica M. Daniel
Temika Powers

POWER OF OBEDIENCE
Durcus Hiller
Jennifer JJ Jones
Crystal C. Cruse

POWER OF DISCIPLINE
Alicia D. Foust
Kenya Posey
Elle Dean

POWER OF FAITH
Dr. Crystal Cooper
Tracy D. Vault
Temeka Miller Thomas
Marvin Craig

KINGDOM PRINCIPLE SECTION INTRODUCTIONS
Patsy Clowney Bloom & Verganell Thomas Craig

REVIEWS

"Where do you want to be in 20 years? We tend to plan for a life we hope to have then justify our plan. The problem with that is, our plan is seldom God's plan. We see and hear what we want, fitting reality into our plan. Many of us faithfully pray every day but never receive an answer from God. It's as if we transmit on one frequency and listen on another. Maybe we need to reprogram our communications equipment so we can send and receive on the same frequency. Dr. J. Le'Ray's compilation of ordinary people recounting their individual journeys from desperation to celebration is filled with transparency and perspective. These testimonies underscore God's eternal presence in our lives, even through our darkest days. While each story is unique, they all describe similar journeys towards renewed faith and understanding of God, all while traveling separate pathways." - **James P. Bell, USA (Retired)**

"The Power of Kingdom Mindset impelled and compelled me to examine my mind and heart. A powerfully authentic masterpiece that is rich with insightful and deeply personal examples of redemption and transformation. A bit of psychological therapy that challenges you to examine your mindset and heart on various godly virtues. It is well documented with biblical scriptures. Reading this book with an open heart can assist with shifting your perspective and help you soar to new heights in your walk with God." - **Juanivi M. Torrence**

Power of Kingdom Mindset evoked so many emotions while promoting a mindset shift throughout. As I read this collection of works I was able to relate, reflect, and begin to work on releasing some of the burdens I carry. The stories included are scripture based, inspiring, and thought provoking. The reflection questions provided in this book were not always easy to digest. I was challenged as I dealt with myself and reminded of how important Faith, Humility, Obedience, and Love are as we journey through life attempting to be reflections of God. This power was a blessing to my soul.
– K. Bellamy-Lloyd, Owner & Executive Director, Modifeye

DEDICATION

This book is dedicated to every Kingdom Citizen to edify the mind, body, and soul. May the stories within accelerate your ascension and catapult you into your divine position in the Kingdom. Here is to unity through transformed and renewed minds. It is all about the build. Let's build together.

ACKNOWLEDGEMENTS

Writing a book is a true blessing. I have had the pleasure of experiencing that blessing a few times since Abba Father directed me to this literary path of writing and publishing. However, compiling a book with 25 authors is an assignment I underestimated in a myriad of ways. The reward has been far beyond what I could ever think or ask. None of this would have been possible if it wasn't for Abba Father trusting me to receive the vision and work diligently to manifest it through the strength of the Holy Spirit. See, this vision was revealed to me in late 2016 and here we are; three years later with an impactful and final product of *the Power of Kingdom Mindset: Volume I* book.

I'm eternally grateful to my husband, Marvin Craig, a co-author in this book, for his agape love, patience, and understanding. He has fought sleep to stay up with me on those many late nights turned early mornings completing tasks for this divine assignment. Though he wanted me to shut it down and rest on several occasions, he supported the press and the pour as I expressed the need to be 'ALL IN' for everyone connected to this book.

After receiving the vision and brainstorming of how to build a model that would assist aspiring authors and others to capture their stories, I had several thoughts. I reached out to Grace Marie Brown, whom showed up on my Facebook timeline, and scheduled a consultation. We connected and I asked several questions about her services as she was only listed as a Ghostwriter in that season. I wanted to figure out how to provide tools and resources to aspiring writers. Those who did not want to physically put pen to paper but would speak into recorders and have content transcribed. We did not finalize any business relationship at that time, yet I continued 'watching' her and eventually contracted her to coach me through my first book, the *Heart 2 Heart Daily Devotional: A 31 Day Transformational Journal.* Thank you so much Grace for your divine guidance and support on so many projects. A very special thank you for your inspiration, encouragement, professionalism, availability, training, and willingness to support me as a book coach while I served as a coach to the twenty-four authors through this process. Your knowledge, authenticity, creativity, and skill are invaluable.

To pastor Jesse Curney III, Senior Pastor of New Mercies Christian Church in Lilburn, Georgia, thank you for reading this book and writing the Foreword. Pastor Curney and First Lady Aleana Curney were my leaders and intricate influencers in my spiritual journey and matriculation. Their shepherding of me and my son throughout some very trying and triumphant seasons, while residing in Georgia from 2001 until 2014, was certainly ordained. As a very busy senior pastor, husband, dad, friend, etc., I know your time is limited, which makes your 'YES' all the more special. The Foreword is dripping with anointing and your blessing on this book truly warmed my heart. Thank you again.

Compiling an anthology book requires a team with like minds and hearts. There are not enough words nor meaning of words to express the gratitude, honor, and blessing I have for all Souls who committed their time, gifts, talents, transparency, vulnerability, courage, skills, resilience, and prayers to manifest this vision. I love and appreciate each and every Co-Author who said 'YES' and shared some very intimate stories in which Abba Father showed up strong and shifted their mindsets in the midst of many trials and tribulations. To the publishing team; Grace of Pen to Publish, mentioned above, Reginald and Candace Blanks of Christlike Graphics for the Power of Kingdom Mindset logos and the anointed book cover, Kristin Bellamy-Lloyd, Owner & Executive Director of Modifeye for her exemplary editing skills and a spirit filled review, and the additional Reviewers; James P. Bell and Juanivi M. Torrence, thank you for your hard work. I would also like to acknowledge a few of the co-authors, Crystal C. Cruse, Ja'Quez D. Cruse, Patsy Clowney Bloom, along with some family members, Kayla Myrie and Donnie Cruse for their service as thought partners, content developers, design reviewers, inspiration, and support during this process. Wow, what a team! To Abba be ALL the GLORY!!!

This was nothing but a divine and ordained occurrence! Someone contacted me and stated that she wanted to support and sponsor an author. Right before she did, I had received a message from an author who wanted to write and share her testimony and was unable to but, she was believing Abba for the provision. She had no idea that I received a message from Deacon Frederick & Latisha Womble seeking to support this assignment by sowing a seed allowing an author to answer 'YES,' without having the burden of covering the fee needed to contribute. My, my, my…Abba is simply amazing and His timing is perfect.

Pastors Kenyon & Jasmine Dudley, leaders of the Church of Acts in Georgia, thank you for sharing your testimonies in your books; *YES in the Dark* and *Finding Courage to Live Free*. The seed for this vision was released and planted before I read your books and reading them surely watered and germinated the seed; all while fertilizing what Abba ordained before sending either of us to this realm. Again, His timing is perfect and I thank each of you for you obedience.

To my intimate and extended supporters, including my family, friends, Sorors of Delta Sigma Theta Sorority Inc., colleagues, teammates on other projects, and social media connections…Thank you for every congratulatory message and prophetic utterance about the impact this literary work will have on the Kingdom.

Lastly, to all Kingdom Citizens, thank you for your obedience as many of you were used at different times, to confirm and reaffirm that I heard what I heard, and saw what I saw in regards to this divine assignment. The sermons, teachings, conversations, and shifts in language that were threaded through those opening their mouths are divinely aligned to this season of transformation and MINDSET SHIFTS.

May divine peace, joy, provisions, clarity, protection, and direction rest upon each of you as we press forward completing each of our divine assignments.

I AM because He IS and YOU are!

TABLE OF CONTENTS

FOREWORD

By: Pastor Jesse Curney III

The Bible declares to us in Philippians 2:5 to "let this mind be in you, which was also in Christ Jesus." I can also remember commercials on television from the United Negro College Fund which told us that, "a mind is a terrible thing to waste," and the anti-drug commercial which suggested that if I took drugs, my brain would fry like an egg. These examples made it clear that the quality of your life is linked to your thinking. If you have a low level of thought and you don't see yourself having a more excellent life; more than likely, the fruit of that shallow thought pattern is also of low quality. However, if you can develop a positive and focused, kingdom mindset, there is no telling what you can accomplish in this world.

In my many years of being in ministry, I have seen people do some incredible things, amidst some horrible circumstances. They succeeded only because they believed there was something better for them and they were not going to let anything stop them from getting all that God had for them.

Throughout scripture, you will find accounts that speak about the importance of a believer having a "Kingdom Mindset." If a person is going to live a prosperous life in God, they must focus their thinking towards beginning to look at things as Christ did.

Having a "Kingdom Mindset" refers to bringing the Kingdom of God here to the earth. Nothing takes place in heaven that does not glorify God. We should want to bring that same glory to God in every aspect of our lives and we should want the same for our lives.

In this book *Power of Kingdom Mindset*, Dr. J. Le'Ray has done a fantastic job of compiling writings from authors who share their stories of how a "Kingdom Mindset" shaped their lives. This book is like opening a treasure chest of life's many challenges, illustrating how the authors overcame their issues by trusting in our Lord and Savior, Jesus Christ.

I was able to identify with many of the stories; how they were able to overcome through believing and standing on the word of God. The internal reflection questions at the end of each chapter will provoke you to explore your mindset and assist you in looking at your circumstances through the lens of Christ.

After reading this book, I am confident that you will find yourself in many of the stories. You will also see how God has been protecting, guiding, and keeping you. You will be encouraged in learning that God wants more for you, but you have to redirect your thinking to the Kingdom of God.

In the Gospel according to Mark, 9th chapter, Jesus is talking to a father who presented his son who has a mute spirit. The father had done all he knew to do and, being at the end of his rope, he brought his son to Jesus. Nothing seemed to be working, and the father was at his wit's end. As the father watched his son convulse violently on the ground, Jesus encouraged the father with these words, "If you can believe, all things are possible to them who believe." The father responded in a way many of us are responding today. He stated with tears in his eyes, "Lord I believe, but help my unbelief." Reading *Power of Kingdom Mindset* will help you strengthen those areas of unbelief you may have and will propel you to live the life God has in mind for you.

Pastor Jesse Curney III

Senior Pastor of New Mercies Christian Church

INTRODUCTION

And do not be conformed to this world [any longer with its superficial values and customs], but be transformed and progressively changed [as you mature spiritually] by the renewing of your mind [focusing on godly values and ethical attitudes], so that you may prove [for yourselves] what the will of God is, that which is good and acceptable and perfect [in His plan and purpose for you].

- Romans 12:2 AMP

Mindset is everything, it is a way of thinking, a disposition, and a frame of mind. Our mindset is critical to our thoughts, choices, responses, reactions, and interactions. Being that mindset is connected to so many factors that shape our everyday life, it is important that we understand how we position ourselves to consistently be true to ourselves about our mindset.

According to Merriam-Webster, mindset is defined as "a mental attitude or inclination; a fixed state of mind." Take a moment to reflect. Is your overall mindset one of positive or negative outlooks? What has shaped your current mindset? Is it based on how you feel or your desires (what you want)? Is it based on your faith? Your beliefs? Your morals and/or your values? These reflective questions are presented to assist us in being true with self, as it relates to where we are in regards to our current state of mind.

A Kingdom Mindset is absolutely necessary for Kingdom Citizens to walk in their ordained power and authority. This is clearly stated in Matthew 6:33 – *"But seek first his kingdom and his righteousness, and all these things will be given to you as well."* Thus, with a Kingdom Mindset leading us, we are aligning ourselves to receive *"all these things"*. Scriptures leading to verse 33 mention a few of *"all these things"*; some being clothes, food, and drink. This passage also speaks to not worrying about anything. Illustrating that there is power in having a Kingdom Mindset.

Just as mindset is everything, so is perspective. A Kingdom Mindset does not only guarantee us our needs in regards to daily or material needs; it provides us with our emotional and spiritual needs as well. These things include peace, joy, happiness, knowledge, understanding, wisdom, and so much more. All of these things are directly correlated to a mindset. Outcomes from life's circumstances are dependent upon our mindset.

This book is filled with short stories of mindset shifts experienced by Kingdom Citizens around a particular Kingdom principle. These stories are personal testimonies in which you will be able to relate to in many ways. The Kingdom principles comprised within are: obedience, truth, love, apology, forgiveness, humility, faith and discipline. There are, at minimum, three different perspectives shared for each mindset.

After reading each story, there are internal reflection questions providing you with a moment to pause, meditate, and capture your reactions and thoughts. These stories share moments of truth, despair, anger, frustration, confusion, lack of self-discipline, low self-esteem, as well as how each author triumphed through the power of their Kingdom Mindset.

Each story is different, yet the same, each person had to journey through, continue to reflect within, and deal with self, all with a courageous spirit. The good news is that all persevered with resilience and can attest that the greatest test was intentionally maintaining a Kingdom Mindset daily. As Romans 12:2 states, *"we are transformed by the renewing of our mind."*

It is important to note that each of these perspectives are personal stories being shared for Abba Father's glory. Moreover, the collaborating authors are not all ordained and licensed clergyman. Why is this important? Because one does not have to be licensed or ordained to share their testimony, nor do they need to be perfect. As it states in Revelation 12:11, *"we overcame and conquered [the devil] because of the blood of the Lamb and because of the word of our testimony, for we did not love our life and renounce our faith even when faced with death."* Read that again.

Our position as Kingdom citizens makes it very clear that the blood, our boldness, and confidence in sharing our testimony is why we overcame. Yes, it is already done. The battle is won! We win! Now, this knowledge should shift our mindset all the more as we journey forth daily knowing that the war is fixed. Our purpose was predetermined before we were formed in our mother's womb and our identity positioned us on the winning side. It is our responsibility to increase our knowledge and apply it as we prepare our souls to return home.

Enjoy the stories, allow them to take root in your heart and embrace the shifts. Thank you for allowing this literary work to speak to your Soul.

Dr. J. Le'Ray, The Compiler

Dr. J. Le'Ray
The HEART Coach

Power of Love

By: Patsy Clowney Bloom & Verganell Thomas Craig

*L*ove is heavily rooted in the character of God. We can love others, and show it through our actions, because God loved us first. God loves you more than you can imagine. And He loves you unconditionally; regardless of your behavior or what you've done.

Agape love is love at the highest level. It's selfless, sacrificial, and unconditional. Love is the high esteem that God has for his human children and the high regard which they, in turn, should have for Him and other people.

There are hundreds of references to love in the Bible, it is certainly the most remarkable book of love in the world. It records the greatest love story ever written – God's unconditional love for us that He sent His son to die on the cross.

Love is God's attributes. Love is also an essential part of His nature. God Is love; He is the personification of perfect love. Such love surpasses our power of understanding. Love like this is everlasting, free, sacrificial, and enduring.

God is love and has demonstrated that love in everything that

He does. Paul compares faith, hope, and love, and concludes that *"the greatest of these is love"*. Our reward for our obedience, as it relates to love, is our blessings in God's timing. It is our duty and obligation to love the Lord our God with all our heart, with all our soul, and with all our mind.

As a child of The Most High, Agape love is our portion. We must continue transforming from the inside, dealing with self, to truly becoming love and journeying as love. Love is what love does.

SCRIPTURE REFERENCES

I Corinthians 12:4-8, John 3:16, Deuteronomy 7:7-8

A NEW KIND OF LOVE

By: Dr. Kelly Bullock Daugherty

I met him in the fall of 1989. I was a senior in high school, and he was a junior. He was quiet, reserved, and stayed very much in the background. I was a little more outgoing and enjoyed attention. I wouldn't have considered him my "type". We grew up very differently, but still had so much in common. We shared the same friends; we both played sports, we loved to laugh and joke with each other, and had a strong sense of value for our families from the beginning. I couldn't pinpoint it at the time, but I knew, there was something about his gentle, yet, bold spirit that drew me towards him. We began dating that fall and were almost inseparable for the entire year.

That next fall, I went away to college in Virginia. I was 18 years old and was certain that I was "in love" at this point. I'm not sure I even knew what love was at that age. What I did know was that I thought of him all the time. I had a funny feeling in my belly whenever I knew I was going to see him and no one else mattered. This had to be what love was all about, right?

People spent so much time trying to discourage our long-distance relationship. I would scoff at them and emphatically exclaim that he and I were different that, "God placed us together for a reason and we would make it!" Eventually, I would stop working so hard to convince others of a love they obviously would never understand. He enrolled in the same college and we remained together as a couple for the next five years.

When I graduated in May 1994, he and I were still an exclusive couple. We certainly had our ups and downs, but I would probably attribute those to growing pains and simply trying to figure life out. Even with all the valleys, we couldn't seem to shake each other. All I could think was that this had to be God's doing. Since I wasn't as close to Christ at that time, I couldn't be that sure, so I simply just tried to continue following my gut and my heart.

After graduation, I went home to be with my parents and found a good job. He had two more years of school and I struggled trying to figure out what to do with my time while he was away. I knew he loved me but being away from him for so long began to cast doubt and insecurities in my mind. Perhaps what people were saying was beginning to reign true. Still, I didn't care what people said. I thought this love was straight from the heavens and continued on the path I thought God had set for me.

In the spring of 1996, he walked the stage, albeit a few credits short of graduation. He left college to help support his family at home. Once life got in the way a bit more, the time to complete those few credits got away from him and he was already deep into the workforce. I understood what was happening and I admired him even more for putting his family ahead of himself. It felt like it took a lot of strength for him to make that decision and I loved him even more through it.

By the spring of 1997, I'd received my graduate degree and was excelling in my job. Suddenly, I wanted more in life. As far as

I was concerned, I was established with two degrees and a good job, but I simply needed more. I'd been with him at this point for almost 8 years. I knew what I wanted, but he was unsure of his next steps. Things between us weren't bad at all, but there was something definitely different. I came to the difficult decision to tell him that I was ready to move on to another phase in my life. I knew I loved him, and I knew I wanted him in my life; I also knew it was time for me to pursue something more than just him. I was planning on moving away to pursue work and further education. I guess in the end it came across as an ultimatum, because in May of 1997, he proposed to me. This *must* be what God had planned for me! I said yes.

We married in June of 1999 and the love we felt seemed straight out of a fairy tale! Marriage came easily for us because we were allowed to be who we were together *all the time*! After about two years, we began working towards starting a family. This, however, didn't come as easily. After a couple of miscarriages, I would discover I was dealing with the inability to conceive a child without medical assistance.

Knowing you are growing a little person in your womb is a love I could have never fathomed before. It's an indescribable kind of love and losing a child before even seeing it, bears an unspeakable disappointment that undoubtedly weighed heavy on my heart. I began to see and hear stories of babies being born to mothers who were unfit, by society's claim, or simply didn't want them. After a third miscarriage, I became confused and enraged to say the least. Here I am, what I believe to be, a God fearing, committed woman; who is married, employed and doing everything considered "right" by society trying to bear a child, and denied three times! God saw more fit to give a child to them and not me? This anger and disappointment did nothing but diminish my mindset into a cluster of negativity and hatred. Not for those other women...but, for God!

I was so angry! A child was obviously not in the cards for us. My husband was suddenly struck with silence in the moment, for fear of saying the wrong thing, in his attempt at being supportive. I would exclaim in anger, *"What kind of God says He loves you and then takes your child right out of your womb??!! If He loved me, we would be pregnant!!"* I began to tear down my temple by filling it with toxins. If God didn't see me and my body fit to carry, why should I honor myself? It was a tough time for me and my husband.

During that time, so many people were rooting for us. I cried many days and nights. We still wanted a child so badly. I finally stopped fighting and submitted to God. I prayed that whenever He saw fit, I would be ready. In the summer of 2001, I would conceive again. This time, the baby would thrive and grow to term. Up until this point, I had resolved that I would never bear children; But God...

In that moment, 1 Corinthians 13: 4-8 (NIV) drew true meaning for me. The verses read as follows:

4 Love is patient, love is kind. It does not envy, it does not boast, it is not proud. 5 It does not dishonor others, it is not self-seeking, it is not easily angered, it keeps no record of wrongs. 6 Love does not delight in evil but rejoices with the truth. 7 It always protects, always trusts, always hopes, always perseveres. 8 Love never fails.

You see, these verses not only bonded my husband and I on our wedding day, but now, bore different meaning as we looked to grow our family. I had wanted so badly to become a mother; my prayers became selfish and demanding. I deserved to be a mother and I felt that God owed it to me since, after all, I was *"doing everything right"*.

In my time of protest, He continued to allow me to rant while giving me signs that I needed to be patient. I needed to learn how to love selflessly, expecting nothing in return. I needed to learn that the gift of a child, was not only a huge responsibility, but a divine sense of accountability. I needed to learn that love was more than simply showing affection. I knew how to do that. What I struggled with was loving like Christ, unconditionally, without inhibitions. This was a difficult and emotional lesson to learn, but also necessary. I was so focused on what other mothers were getting that I lost touch with Christ. I lost touch with myself and I was spiritually convicted. That day I stopped fighting and submitted to Him, was the day He would deem me ready for the responsibility of a child.

In March 2002, we would give birth to our first son. I would call him my first Blessing from God. Two more Blessings followed and made our family complete. Unlike my earlier experiences, I would now have the opportunity to appreciate love like never before. The love of a faithful, merciful God, who, in all my doubt, never turned His back nor left me. This new kind of love, God's love, made me feel whole again and I would promise to share with the world how this new-found love changed my mind and my life.

INTERNAL REFLECTIONS QUESTIONS:

1 Corinthians 13: 4-8 (NIV) defines the love of Christ. In what aspect of your life has He shown you unselfish and faithful love?

_____

_____

_____

_____

_____

Have you ever found that your own expectations of love kept you from experiencing the true love of Christ? How did you surrender to His love in those moments?

_____

_____

_____

_____

_____

In surrendering to God's love, how did your life change? How has this impacted your outlook on life and life's challenges?

_____

_____

_____

_____

_____

KEY LOVE FROM ABOVE

By: Dani Keys

October 9, 2001, holds the tale of a happily married 24-year-old woman named Danielle Vaughn. She was a highly intelligent top producer and youngest manager ever of the telephone company where she was employed. Things were going along very well, according to the all-American storybook fairy tale dream; until, 6:13 pm that day when everything changed.

The day was so special. I was receiving my 13th customer service award and I was the only one to ever receive that many in one single year. I was beyond excited to share the news with my husband. I left work a little bit earlier than normal that day because I was 6 months pregnant and had a doctor's appointment.

I decided to stop by my husband's job to share the great news and wanted to surprise him. I arrived at the parking lot right as his lunch hour began. But the surprise was mine, as I saw my husband kissing another co-worker. WOWZER!

How did I miss this? What did I do? What didn't I do? Why is everything spinning upside down right now like a bad carnival ride? Somebody, PLEASE tell me I am dreaming! I refuse to end up a divorce statistic like my parents. Nope! Not me.

COMPILED BY DR. J. LE'RAY

I wanted my kids to have both parents, I was a Proverbs woman. I knew what it said in Proverbs 11:29, *"Whoever brings ruin on their family will inherit only wind, and the fool will be servant to the wise".* I was so determined that I was not going to be the one that ruined my family that I continued to stay with him over the next couple of years. But, as it turns out, the prince charming of this story, decided he needed nine more Cinderella's in his life so, I was forced to divorce.

This was a hard time and place for me. I went from being happily married with a family, employed, making a six-figure income to a divorced, depressed, broken, and broke single mother of 3 children under the age of 4 years old living off welfare. Though none of this was easy I pressed through like the woman in Proverbs 9:1 (NKJV), *"Wisdom hath builded her house, she hath hewn out her seven pillars".*

I knew that I had to start relying on wisdom and understanding so that the past couldn't take me into my future. I had to constantly remind myself that even in the darkest of times, a star will still glow for the people to see it. Its purpose is meant to naturally glow and light the way for others. This reminded me of the scripture Matthew 5:14 *"Ye are the light of the world. A city that is set on a hill cannot be hid".* I kept going about trying to mend together the shattered pieces of my life.

One day I took my daughter Dezaraye to the doctor, she was 3 years old, to seek help as to why she was delayed in her motor skills. The doctor came back with the most shocking words that changed my life *"Ms. Vaughn, the results from all the test we have done are conclusive and your daughter has Cerebral Palsy. Unfortunately, she will need ongoing care from our specialist as she will never have the ability to walk or talk like a normal girl".*

As I looked towards him with tears streaming down my face, I thought to myself *"Never walk nor talk?" "How can this be?"* I picked up my children and raced out of that office and never returned to that doctor.

I kept thinking about this diagnosis for the next two weeks. During this period, I was so depressed I literally did not eat one single thing; I began to feel weak and lightheaded. I began remembering some of the biblical word I had been taught in church. I remembered praying and reading the word. I started with just one scripture, then one chapter, and the one thing that I started doing that I couldn't seem to stop doing was talking. Many people these days call the type of talking I was doing an "intercessory prayer warrior."

I started just talking to the walls, the ceiling, and doors. I started going into my daughters room and just crying (yet still talking), and I would start fixing her pillow so that her head would be more comfortable, at the same time I was talking to that pillow saying something along the lines of *"I'm fixing this pillow so that when your voice is fixed it will be rested on a comfortable pillow."* I would straighten her blankets and say something along the lines of *"I'm gonna straighten this blanket out for you so when GOD straightens out your walking your legs will be warm"*

I just kept talking to GOD like He was right next to me. Every single day in my prayers before reading the Word I would ask for the gift of love and giving. I asked GOD for these specific gifts because I was afraid that my daughter would not be loved enough by the rest of the world. The struggles just kept coming. I thought maybe this was a sign that I just had not prayed enough. I started kicking my prayers into overdrive because, over the next few years, I learned that my older son

Drew was on the autism spectrum, had Aspergers mixed with a bit of Prader-Willi syndrome.

I kept thinking to myself – *"Why me? I prayed? I was a good person? What did I do to deserve all these challenges?"* Now I had two children that had constant medical and academic issues. I would secretly say to myself *"just be thankful it's two and not all three Dani."* But I spoke too soon! BOOM! Is this a horrible joke? Nope. No Joke.

I learned in a very traumatic way that my youngest son Donnie had a heart disease, called prolonged QT, and if that wasn't enough, he also had an oppositional defiant disorder. Later, Dezaraye was also diagnosed with pica and deafness. Holy Moly! I really did think to myself, *"who did this to me? Can I cancel this life and get a refund? Hold on, you mean to tell me that GOD doesn't have an exchange policy?"*

However, my faith kept me going even though it was not easy. It was like playing in the Love Olympics daily without ever getting the award or the metal. After a really long chit chat with God for the next week, I had a dream that kept coming to me night after night. In the dream, I would hear Proverbs 3:15 - *"She is more precious than rubies, And nothing you can wish for compares with her [in value]."*

So, here I was, a single mother of three special needs children, of differing disabilities, simply acting on a dream that I couldn't get out of my head nor heart. I felt the pressing need to create a company as a resource for other single parents to help add value to the journey for others with my own experiences.

The Word says to write the vision and make it plain in Habakkuk 2:2. *"And the LORD answered me, and said, Write the vision, and make it plain upon tables, that he may run that readeth it".* Pastor, Dr. Kelvin Morgan, always had a saying *"find a need, fill it; find a hurt, heal it."* Mom would say to me *"feel"* the holy ghost fire in your belly rise when you do. Within the next seven days I did just as she told me to do.

I began a journey of self-love which, in fact, was the hardest of all the love trials. You see, I found it naturally easy to love others but, difficult to love what was in that mirror. I had to identify myself in the mirror. What I saw was hard and uncomfortable to love. I had been so consumed by the external factors of life. With struggles of marriage, divorce, finances, children, disabilities, society, friends, and family; I lost my own identity. Where did I go? Could I be found? How do I find ME? Am I important? I felt like somehow, I'd probably drifted off into the misty air somewhere. If not, I had hoped I did.

Would I ever love that unrecognizable person looking back at me in that mirror? One day I ventured out walking, minding my own business, and I stumbled across a man who would forever change my life. He was able to answer that previous question. He seemed a bit familiar. You see he had this trustworthy sense about him that just kept drawing me closer to him. Every word he spoke seemed like it was something my own father would say to me. I felt like he had been at all of my holidays and birthdays.

He was so wise and profound with his wisdom and understanding. Suddenly it hit me it was my Father! ABBA! *"Father it is you!"* I cried out. *"I am so lost. I am so confused. I need you. Guide me. Let me stand in your Privilege of Power."* As I continued to cry out, I felt a SHIFT in my own vocal sound. I just continued to cry, wailing out loud *"Beneficent LOVE & Privilege of Power GOD"* until I fell asleep.

The next day, I felt the strongest urge to race to Dezaraye's bedside. When I arrived, there she was with her glowing tan skin, brown eyes, and long brown hair; looking a bit like Pocahontas, smiling up at me with the biggest smile. Then she pointed to her chest area, close to her heart, and out of her mouth made a sound *"wub"*.

Wait? Could this be? Really? Did this just happen? Am I dreaming? The doctor said my daughter would never talk. Did my daughter just attempt to point to her heart and say, love? Did Dezaraye make the connection of love? Love is the key after all right? GOD can do all things, right? It was indeed true. Day after day, little by little, my sweet Dezaraye started displaying a communication connection with me through a variety of vocal prompts, sign language and even guessing.

I knew, because of what God had done for me, that I had to give hope to other moms too. I realized that my daughter's testimony was important. I knew that there was an anointing that was on our lives. I had no clue where to start I just knew I had to. I stayed up late nights after the kids had gone to bed and I started searching for the current resources and services for moms. Seeing the lack of support I became a huge advocate.

I was not as frustrated by the lack of programs available to the children, but more so by their coordination efforts with single moms like myself. I did as GOD said, I created a company for moms to provide first, LOVE OF SELF education, knowledge, and learning. Then, structure, community, and understanding. Bringing together parents of children with special needs, I wanted to help empower them into realizing their dreams. The fact is, even with their hardships, they can accomplish whatever they and their children desire. They too can lead a rich and fulfilling lives regardless of having a disability.

Since 2016, I, Dani Keys has been able to offer many programs for both families of children with special needs and to the public. My daughter, sons, and I have continued to blaze the trail through creating new opportunities, awareness, and cultivating a space for others to move into their abilities to see how they are connecting to the KEY LOVE FROM ABOVE.

It is so easy for me to tell myself *"you are great"* but to *"FEEL GREAT"* is so different. Now, I force myself to do things I wouldn't normally do; all the time. If it makes me feel comfortable, I challenge myself to change it. I have taught myself that makeup doesn't make me pretty. I have taught myself that the word LOVE is not a unicorn. It does exist.

Now you, challenge yourself, feel uncomfortable, make a change, find the word LOVE in you.

INTERNAL REFLECTION QUESTIONS:

Do you find yourself always believing the professionals over your own intuition as a parent? If so Why? Why not? Does this alter your beliefs about GOD's love?

_____

_____

_____

_____

_____

During this story, Dani and her love for her children were the leaders; but her disability of love and Dezaraye were the influencers.   Have you encountered times where the people with the leadership titles are not the actual influencers within your own communities?

_____
_____
_____
_____
_____

What was the most valuable lesson you learned from this story?

_____
_____
_____
_____
_____

LOVE-AUGUSTA SIGHTS

By: Toni Brown

I t's been explained that love is a sensitivity to emotional affection from one person to another. This was a statement a high school friend shared with me that was foundational in shaping my perspective as to what love was. Being that I was raised by my grandmother (Lord rest her soul) and sheltered from my things of "the world", this was my reference point for quite some time about love. Boy was I naïve and totally wrong. As God guided me through my darkest days with that mindset about love, I discovered the importance of meditation of scriptures that saw me through to agape love. As an only child growing up without a father, I learned to relish in statements from men that were not always valid or even true. As time progressed and I entered my 20's as an inexperienced adult with many unhealthy experiences with "love", I had learned to view "love" as a false word without a true definition.

As time went on, I began to understand what I needed in a man. Well, at least that's what I'd said to myself. I never prayed and asked God what His will was for my life, but I always told God what I wanted expecting Him to give me my heart's desires.

In the fall of 1990, I began dating someone in college that lasted for well over twenty years. I was in love, right? No, I was in the worst battlefield that my mind, soul, and sanity than I could ever imagine. For several years, I stayed in a toxic relationship because it was the only real relationship I'd ever experienced. I stayed because I had children with a man who wanted my body, but never our children. I stayed because I wanted my boys to know who their father was.

This was "LOVE" in my mind until the voice of God spoke to me through an explicit dream. In October of 2011 I began my spiritual transformation. God revealed to me that the young man with whom I had a relationship for over twenty years was NOT the man that he'd selected for me. God also stated to me that for him to send my future husband, that He created and prepared for me, I had to end the toxic relationship. This was not an easy task, but I continued to trust God and meditate on His Word.

God not only strengthened me but provided me with a way out by teaching overseas for two years with my children. This was the start of My-Rebirth! Joshua 1:9 states, *Have I not commanded you? Be strong and courageous. Do not be afraid; do not be discouraged, for the LORD your God will be with you wherever you go."*

It was on a Saturday, the end of January 2015, that I was formally introduced to Mr. Augusta Sights through an online profile. Augusta Sights was a gentle and kind man who I didn't know how to appreciate when we first began communicating online. This lack of appreciation was derived from my past experiences with the word, love.

Weekly, I would log in to my profile to see what was new. I know you're probably wondering what site I'm referring to; Well, it was an online dating site in which I've known people who have discovered true love. I'll never forget the moment Augusta Sights expressed his interest in me and often texted me early in the morning to say, "good morning and have a blessed day."

I was so nervous and very apprehensive of this new-found conversation with a man I hardly even knew. Immediately, after communicating with him often, I quickly began to shy away from him. Deliberately not being available for his online interactions, texts, or phone calls. You see, as a woman full of past rejections, hurt, and loneliness, I felt as though I couldn't appreciate what was in front of me. Often, I would ask myself, *"How is it that life can sabotage our views about someone who may be the right one for us?"* The answer to this question during my season of being blinded was that I believed all men were liars, cheaters, and women were used as drop off deposits of pleasure! As I grew spiritually, I realized that if I continued to expound on what was not destined in Gods eyes, life would continue to sabotage my views. This type of mindset could ultimately cost you to miss out on God blessing for your life. I am grateful for my mind shifting in this regard.

Ecclesiastes 3-8 states that there is a time to love and a time to hate, a time for war and a time for peace. I meditated on the scripture, prayed, and questioned God concerning my new friend. God intervened and laid on my heart, without hesitation, that this time everything was going to be pleasing. A few weeks later, I reached out to Augusta Sights; he responded without hesitation, filled with excitement. *"Where have you been stranger?"* From that moment we talked and laughed the night away.

Even though we were exhausted the next day from the all-night stimulating conversation, we both continued to text each other throughout the day. Augusta Sights was in the U.S. Army, stationed in Augusta, Ga. I live a two-hour drive away, on the South side of Atlanta. Each day for over a year we communicated, but we'd never physically met. There were days that I often wondered if I was ready for a relationship that could end up being more than just friends, but again I remembered *Ecclesiastes 3…A Time for Everything.*

It was June 29, 2016, and the time had finally come for Augusta Sights and I to meet. I was overjoyed with excitement but wanted to remain calm, I mean this was our first-time meeting. While driving to Augusta, I meditated on the sweet gospel sounds of artists who ministered to my soul. I soon realized that God was ministering to me through His music. Once the tears were wiped away and my make-up reapplied, I was entering Augusta.

Mr. Augusta Sights and I were to meet at Red Lobster at 12 pm sharp. At this point, I had several feelings tingling through by body. Palms sweating, lips vibrating, and heart pulsating with anticipation as Augusta Sights appeared from his vehicle. The pulsation of my heart palpitating was the true indicator of the excitement built for the unknown man whom I had been in contact with for over a year; but had never seen face to face. It was a heart to heart connection for sure.

Out of nowhere, Augusta Sights appeared in uniform and with a bouquet of flowers. I can't really remember how long we stayed and laughed at the restaurant, but it felt as though we had known each other for years. Once the weekend ended, we both decided that we had feelings for each other that went beyond just friendship. I was very nervous, as I was in a previous relationship that I considered to be promising but it was again not of God's will. I'd remember praying and asking God to reveal to me a sign if this wasn't His will for my life. If it wasn't, I'd asked God to remove this man from my life as I did nor want to experience another toxic relationship. I only desired to submit to His will for my life. I'd concluded that doing things my way was never good, and that it would only continue to bring dysfunction into my life and my home.

It took Augusta Sights and, I being led by God, exactly six months to realize that we were not lusting for each other. We were in love. On July 17, 2017, at 9:00 AM, in the presence of God, Mr. Augusta Sights and I were joined in Holy Matrimony. Today, Mr. Augusta Sights, my husband, is known to me as my "Blue Skies" but known to others as my "Boaz". On that day in July, I experienced what God intended for all his children to experience- Love.

Love today is defined, from my perspective, as a devoted action that you show your loved one continuously. If you ever thought God wasn't listening to your prayers, just know He is. 1 Corinthians 13:4-5 says,

Love is patient, love is kind, it doesn't envy, it doesn't boast, it is not proud, it doesn't dishonor others, it is not self-seeking, it is not easily angered, it keeps no records of wrong.

As you ponder over this scripture, ask yourself these questions: What are you willing to change in order to receive and experience love? Are you willing to follow God's will or continue waiting for your own will to be done? Are you willing to accept continued pain, loneliness, and anger?

I elected to let go, and let God have full control over my life and my heart. Due to God's will and my obedience to His word, I am able to receive and reciprocate love. Accepting God's promises over my life has produced the results of a happy marriage.

Allow God's will into your everyday life, and you will see that true love will find you in God's perfect timing. I'm very thankful to God for humbling me and preparing me for the blessing of true love which ultimately led me to become a wife. Love God and yourself first, keeping all of his commandments close to your heart.

INTERNAL REFLECTION QUESTIONS:

Do I battle the fears of yesterday or move on with today, even though I do not know the outcome of tomorrow?

_____

_____

_____

_____

_____

What are you willing to change in order to receive and experience love?

_____

_____

_____

_____

_____

Are you willing to follow God's will or continue your own?

_____

_____

_____

Power of Humility

By: *Patsy Clowney Bloom & Verganell Thomas Craig*

After reading definitions and scripture about the meaning of humility and reflecting on our life experiences, humility can be defined as: 1) the state of being humble 2) freedom from pride and arrogance, 3) humbleness of mind; 4) a deep sense of one's' own unworthiness in the sights of God, 5) not self-absorbent, 6) repentant for sin, and 7) submission to the divine will of God. Before honor is humility; true humility is to bow oneself to the spirit's leading and the result of having some wisdom. Some intuition of all human traits, but we have to bring them into subjection to God's will and recognizing that our worth comes from God alone. According to *Proverbs 18:12 (GNT), No one is respected unless he is humble; arrogant people are on the way to ruin.* This clearly shows why there must humility before there is honor.

Humility is admitting you might not be the best in everything. Humility is commanded by God and useful in our social life. Those who possess it are heard by God. They can recognize their faults. They are grateful, and not don't boast based on what they have. Being humble also means you are able to admit when you are wrong. In conversation, humility allows you to be more considerate; embarrassing others, yet appreciating them and listening to their ideas.

Humility allows us to compliment others on their achievements with a pure heart. If we can be a bit more open minded to others' ideas, we would be able to appreciate them more than ever. We need to be humble to experience respectable relationships in our lives. This truth amplifies the fact that the physical being is as small as a speck of dust and nothing without the Holy Spirit. Upon knowing and embracing this truth, the character of humility becomes a lifestyle yielding advance.

To be humble one knows that they are no better than the next reflecting in our words and actions. The power in humility is amplified when we are intentional to honor others and not ourselves. Our honor comes from our consistent lifestyle of humility.

SCRIPTURE REFERENCES

Micah 6:8, Ephesians 4:2, Philippians 2:3

HUMILITY BECOMES ADVANCE

By: Ja'Quez D. Cruse

I was alone, no family that were relatives, just me and my decisions. I was working at Subway, making eight dollars an hour, making eleven dollars an hour. I was driving a car gifted to me, no legit home, with twins on the way. I was working eighteen-hour days, six days a week. This continued for about two months as I found places to lay my head daily.

One early morning, I was on my way to open the store and fell asleep behind the wheel. I woke up just as my vehicle was running off the road. Once my truck jumped the curb I woke up and grabbed the wheel just in time, I nearly a light pole. I swerved into the middle of a busy four-lane road and blew out all tires before coming to a stop. This was nothing less than a wake-up call. The flow of blessings and tests had just begun.

At the top of 2015 my greatest accomplishment was the birth of two beautiful baby girls. At the time of my twin's birth, I was twenty-one years young. Graced with a place to live, by their overwhelmingly generous maternal grandparents, I was welcomed into their home. I was treated like family. I embraced that love since I had no family of my own nearby.

I was no longer without consistent comfortable living conditions. I was no longer without a vehicle, and most importantly I was always with my children. While living in this home I struggled to maintain employment. Honestly, I took my situation and my position in my new living conditions for granted. There was no discipline in my movements or choices. I went into a place where pleasing myself was my only concern because I knew my children were well taken care of. I learned early you get out exactly what you put in, in this world. The effort that I put into a situation was exactly what I was going to get out of it. I knew this, but as I did what I wanted to do, this lesson was not in the forefront of my mind. Then, the tests began. Things were being presented to tempt me, and these tests were coming back to back. I was failing each of these tests with flying colors as I was doing what I wanted to do. My decisions when tempted were not aligned to a Kingdom Mindset.

On June 15th, 2015 my beautiful baby girls were dedicated back to the Lord. On June 16th, 2015 my life was spared as I stared down the barrel of a 45 caliber pistol that jammed. The Lord intervened in my time of need despite my irrational decisions and unholy motives. I was done failing tests!

That began a series of choices that could only benefit me and my family – a perspective-shifting season. All I wanted was life and joy for my family. I had been humbled on a new level and was now standing on faith stronger than ever before. Moving forward I knew there was a great purpose for my life. I began to focus on the development of my children and my spirit man.

I was on the search for employment, catching gigs here and there, but nothing consistent or enough to provide for a family of four. I found myself at a state job fair only after driving someone else there. I waited for so long that I decided to go in myself, *"what's the worst that could happen"* I told myself. I was placed in the exam room and aced the test. I went through to the panel interview and felt right at home. There were no nerves, just being myself. After the interview, the interviewers had a verbal dispute as to whose office I would be in. This was exactly what I needed. Not only to reassure myself that I was on the right path; but also to begin to set the foundation for my family.

The great feeling did not last long because shortly thereafter my family and I are involved in a hit and run. It was a traumatic experience for everyone involved, we were all blessed to have no major injuries; just a totaled vehicle and very upset children. This new journey was surely full of more tests.

Being the nice guy that I am, I was doing a favor for a friend who had legal issues of their own. It was an early Friday morning and I was to take my friend's daughter to school in his car. Little did I know, the tag was different on this out of state vehicle and unfortunately for me, I was pulled over by a Sherriff. I received three separate tickets before making it to the school. Humbled by God's grace and mercy, each citation was thrown out when I went to court. I was unemployed for about five months living every day knowing that my break was coming.

I started working at the new job on January 3rd. I was elated that this thing was actually about to happen. This career path was one I found myself in, my talents and leadership qualities were exposed effortlessly. I had been so humbled, that these blessings felt more like miracles. This job allowed me to purchase my first car, in my name, after working for six months. Within eight months, I was in a place where my family and I could move and stand on our own.

My humility had become advance, the Lord blessed my obedience. I have come to realize that life is about cycles. Cycles full of tests where we are only tested through our own temptations. This new career was truly an eye-opening and life-changing opportunity. I was experiencing paid for trips, rentals, and travel reimbursement – something completely new to me. At one point, I began to get unfocused again; not realizing all that was at stake. Once again, taking my situation and my position for granted. I slowly realized that the career was seasonal – a stepping stone – a place where the Lord allowed me to see myself on many different levels.

As we live and progress in life, be it personally, spiritually, or in our careers, we will experience great responsibility as the tests are passed. Passing the tests equips and positions us for the next level. The Lord continued to test me and show me who I was in different situations. I was in a professional environment for the first time and learning how to conduct myself accordingly. There are always going to be distractions set in place, but it is our duty to recognize these distractions and avoid them. This task is most certainly easier said than done, but one that is pivotal in advancing both life and mindset.

In this stage of my life, I began to realize the importance of consistency in prayer and acting on those things I prayed for. James 2:14 says, *What does it profit a man if someone says he has faith but does not have works.* That scripture motivated me and I began to apply for different jobs. I was called back for an interview with the Department of Juvenile Justice. I was excited. I saw some light at the end of this tunnel. My faith was tested again and not knowing why, at the time, I was not selected for the position. This was all for my good.

With a smiling face, I returned to work where there was a daily battle. The antagonism had become more persistent. I was shifted from team to team, daily duties changed, even seating arrangements changed. The overall stability of the job was undefined. The systems being used to complete tasks were in constant dysfunction. On a large scale, there was no balance or effective communication which caused chaos amongst everyone involved. Knowing that I could only control me and deal with what I could day by day, I began to put all hinges that were notably out of order in writing. I even went as far as putting a formal demotion request in explaining how my certifications could allow a smoother transition from lobby to service.

Once that request was denied by my superiors, I continued showing up to work daily with a smile on my face. Although I did not understand the why behind the no. I consulted a senior worker in the office seeking some insight and clarity. The senior worker advised me to go to my Human Resource representative. I requested a meeting and attended with all of the correspondence I had sent to management and my other coworkers in an effort to make clear the challenges I was experiencing on my job. The next day, I was terminated.

In hindsight, I was warned by many of my coworkers that the series of events that I was experiencing was similar to a termination path. So, I was sort of prepared mentally when the termination occurred. I had peace with the termination as I was advocating for what was right. The implications from this termination were plentiful, varied with ripple effects through my home as it related to provisions for day to day living.

I was back to square one, with no job and a continuous cycle of responsibilities, BUT GOD. I was aware of these cycles, this was very similar to a previous season in my life. I had lived this cycle of uncertainty and unemployment a time or two at this point in my life. At the beginning of 2019, I decided to do things differently. I got rid of all the things I saw as distractions. For the first time in my life, I decided to truly fast and stay grounded in prayer. While doing so, I began to see layers of breakthroughs for me. I found inner peace and energy that could allow my focus to be complete. A clear mind is the land of infinite possibilities.

I completed my first devotional during the first thirty-one days of the year and that was proof to myself that I could commit to anything I wanted to with love and focus. Psalm 149:4 — *For the Lord takes Delight in his people; he crowns the humble with victory.* This scripture has taken a stronghold on my spirit, and it makes me hold myself accountable every day. I truly believe that the fear of the Lord is the beginning of wisdom and humility becomes advance.

INTERNAL REFLECTION QUESTIONS:

How is the principle of humility showing up in your mindset and life?

_____

_____

_____

_____

_____

Has humility advanced you in any way?

_____

_____

_____

_____

_____

Has humility been a hindrance in your life?

_____

_____

_____

_____

_____

HE HUMBLED ME IN THE WORKPLACE

By: Nikki T. Tibbs

*I*n May 2008, as a single mother and at 32 years of age, I walked across a stage to receive my Bachelor of Science in Psychology with a minor in Business Administration. At the time, I was working a full-time job in IT, as a Team Lead, but was ready to move onto something new.

In August 2008, I began a job in a completely different field and never looked back. My job title was Program Analyst, which was a catch-all for all things program management related. During the next 2 ½ years, I was exposed to many areas, professionally, that really piqued my interest, only to decide that I wanted to move on to a job that would allow me to work in two specific areas.

In February 2011, God blessed me with the exact job for which I had prayed, as a Master Scheduler. The next 8 years in this position would teach me and grow me quite a bit. The first 2 years in this new role were extremely stressful. As a matter of fact, I spent the first 2 years trying to get out. I even submitted my resignation 11 months after my start date, only to be encouraged by my teammates and Human Resources to stay.

I faced several challenges during the first 2 years, many of which fed my insecurities in this new role. Honestly, I felt like a fraud. I felt like I didn't know what I was doing, and why I was there. I felt ill-equipped and unable to keep up with the fast pace.

In mid-2013 I began working with a Program Manager named Cal, who would become a friend over the course of the next 5 years. I remember interviewing him for the job, and I liked that he was very honest about why he was in the job market. I also liked that he seemed very interested and excited about working for the company. Once he was hired and in the door, it appeared that he was going to be a great fit.

In 2015, I had finally gotten into a rhythm in my role. I still had my insecurities, but I continued to work through them. Over the years I had received great performance reviews, won awards, received great raises, bonuses, received many kudos, and pats on the back for a job well done.

In April 2015, there were management changes on one of the projects I supported, which caused me to work more closely with Cal than I had in the previous 2 ½ years. After his boss was fired, Cal took over the role, which put him in a position to have more responsibility, accountability and decision-making ability. At first, I was excited to work with Cal, because he was a breath of fresh air compared to his predecessor. He appeared to be up for the challenge and ready to make some much needed positive changes on the project.

I found out very quickly that the change I had hoped for wasn't going to happen. I saw a different side of Cal. He was very arrogant and stubborn, had no self-awareness, and just wouldn't allow me to do my job. Every interaction with Cal was a challenge. His controlling nature allowed him to believe that he could handle everyone's role on the project.

I wasn't the only one on the team who had this type of experience or interaction with him. Early on, I communicated my concerns, which were always met with lip service. He would say he understood the issues and that he'd work on them. He never fixed the issues. In fact, he got progressively worse as the demands on the project intensified. The types of issues I ran into with Cal included being undermined, spoken to with anything other than respect, and a simple lack of appreciation for the role I played on the project.

In 2017, I had reached my breaking point with Cal. While working on a proposal, he decided to be more hands-on with my role, he attempted to partially take it over, although he had no previous experience. The expectation was that I would clean up and make pretty anything that he did incorrectly or ruined. Keep in mind, I was in a constant battle with my own insecurities with respect to my job duties, despite my many successes over the years.

For weeks, we had shouting matches as I explained to him his mistakes and that he was causing me more work in the clean-up than if I were to handle the job myself. Out of sheer frustration and anger, I began to take a passive-aggressive approach with Cal throughout the completion of the proposal.

I stopped providing the guidance, knowing there were problems with what he was doing. I began to become an unavailable resource, leaving him to figure it out on his own. It wasn't the most Christ-like approach, but I was at my wit's end and was tired of the blatant disrespect. Eventually, he would start to throw me under the bus to others on the team, and I reciprocated by explaining to those same teammates that I wasn't part of the process due to Cal insisting on handling the process himself.

Between battling my own insecurities and battling Cal's inability to let me do my job, which ultimately fed my insecurities, I realized that I couldn't keep going in circles with him over this project and any other project where I was his support. I also realized that I had been seething for approximately 3 years. Enough was enough and I had to find a better way.

In January 2018, after continuous cycles of anger, and arguments and passive aggressiveness, I fasted. I fasted for an entire month, concentrating on many areas in my life, but namely the anger and frustration and how I had been handling myself at work. I fasted from TV and social media. Each night I came home and dove into scripture and immersed myself into praise and worship music. The tears flowed, and the lightbulbs came on as I spent time with God, seeking wisdom, and peace and how to move forward.

At the start of the fast, to shift my focus I held onto Psalms 46:10 (NLT) *"Be still and know that I am God! I will be honored by every nation. I will be honored throughout the world."* Throughout the fast, I researched scripture on anger which eventually led me to scripture on humility and forgiveness. In studying anger scriptures, I realized that I had allowed the anger to control me and my interactions with not only Cal but everyone else I worked with.

Ephesians 4:26 (NLT) states, *"And don't sin by letting anger control you. Don't let the sun go down while you are still angry…"* Out of anger I was foolish and provided petty responses to the situation. Proverbs 29:11 (NLT) reminded me that, *"fools vent their anger, but the wise quietly hold it back."* I needed to learn to be quick to listen and slow to speak when it came to Cal. James 1:19 guided me to *"understand this, my dear brothers and sisters: You must all be quick to listen, slow to speak, and slow to get angry."* My insecurities played a role in how fast I tuned Cal out.

Looking back, I understand that Cal was under pressure from those he reported to, and it wasn't that he thought I couldn't do the job. His way of coping with the pressure coming from above was to assert more control. I happened to take it as a personal attack when it wasn't. The verse, Proverbs 18:12 (KJV) states, *"Pride goeth before destruction, and a haughty spirit before a fall."* This really stuck out to me during my fast. I didn't want to be this prideful person who alienated people at work, or worse, someone who lost their job because they were so concerned about fighting with a co-worker.

Eventually, God would also let me see that Proverbs 18:12 wasn't just for me but was also for Cal. I realized that I had to humble myself and try to see Cal the way God saw him. That would be the only way for me to proceed with the working relationship, and it would be the only way to remove the anger. I repented and asked God for forgiveness for how I had played out the situation. I also thanked Him for giving me the clarity and the wisdom to see that I was going down the wrong path; how to move forward with the fast; and how to handle the situation with Cal after the fast. I needed to proceed with a humble heart, patience, and a gentle word. *"Since God chose you to be the holy people he loves, you must clothe yourselves with tenderhearted mercy, kindness, humility, gentleness, and patience."* (Colossians 3:12 NLT)

At the completion of the fast, I scheduled some time with Cal. I requested some time with him, late in the afternoon, knowing that many would have left work for the day and the atmosphere would be a bit more relaxed. We grabbed an empty office, closed the door and I started in with a humble heart. I led with an apology for the last several years of arguments and miscommunication. I explained my own insecurities, and how they played a role in my reactions to how Cal wanted to work with me. I finished up by saying I wanted to move forward in a more positive way; in a way that would allow us the ability to collaborate.

As we talked, I could feel the hostility between us melt away. He apologized and explained away his own insecurities and frustrations. He also expressed great respect for me and what I do, and that he never meant to minimize my role. I also found out that day that he was fairly new in Christ. My God!

I'm currently in year 8, 2019, and my working relationship with Cal has improved drastically. There are still some challenges, but each time I hit a roadblock, I just remember to humble myself, not take it personally, and do my best to support Cal. The blessing to come out of this situation is that I've been able to put into practice what I learned about humility.

I've had another situation at work where, for many years, I felt as if I was in competition with a teammate because we have the same job duties. We are the only two employees in the company with our skillset responsible for supporting the entire company. After my scenario with Cal, I realized that my insecurities also played a role in my relationship with my teammate Doug. So, I had a very similar conversation with him, coming to him humbly and explaining my insecurities and that I'd like to move forward and learn from each other. The outcome of that conversation with Doug was favorable. We now have a better understanding of each other. I also believe it's helped us to support the company's needs and each other.

I've also been able to apply this kingdom principle in my personal life with family. Recently, my beautiful daughter Alicia turned 21 and I felt led to have a conversation about our history. As we all know there is only one perfect person; one perfect parent, and that surely isn't me! I made many mistakes during my daughter's teenage years, and I felt led to talk through those mistakes with her and to apologize for those mistakes.

When Alicia was 15, she snuck someone she was seeing, Devon, into the house. Devon was someone I didn't care for and thought was a horrible influence on my daughter. Once they were caught, I walked Devon out. Then I put my hands on my daughter out of anger and frustration, and then I walked her out of the house as well.

At the time, with the help of my mother and sister, we found Alicia and brought her back home that night. Eventually, we worked through this situation, but I never forgot how bad I felt for having reacted the way that I did. Even more importantly, I never wanted this to be something she carried with her for the rest of her life thinking that I was okay with my behavior. I didn't want this to be a stumbling block in her adult life, and I didn't want it to influence how she raises my grandchildren when she has kids of her own.

So, I felt that I needed to address it and let her know how sorry I was. I called my daughter, as she attends college out of state, and I started in with a humble heart as I did in the other two scenarios. I let her know that I love her and explained why I reacted the way that I did and that I'm not proud of the way I handled our situation. I also let her know that it was important to me that she knows my reaction was inappropriate and that I don't want it to hinder our relationship. I didn't want it to weigh on her life moving forward.

Through humility, I believe we can make course corrections, changing the trajectory of our relationships. Through humility, I was able to improve my relationships at work, allowing for a more collaborative and supportive environment. Also, through humility, I was able to improve my relationship with my daughter, allowing for a more open and honest relationship as adults, and as mother and daughter.

INTERNAL REFLECTION QUESTIONS:

What situation(s) in your life, past or present, is currently causing you stress, anger and/or anxiety? How is this situation(s) impacting your life?

_____

_____

_____

_____

_____

Do you think humbling yourself can help to resolve your situation(s)? If yes, why? If no, why not?

_____

_____

_____

_____

_____

Using the Power of Humility, what steps could you take to bring about resolution?

_____

_____

_____

_____

_____

THE HONOR IN HUMILITY

By: Alicia D. Foust

*W*hen I was 9 years old I expressed a desire to play the piano. My father asked me why and I told him I wanted to play for church. So, he signed me up for piano lessons. I was so excited. After I learned the basics I would go home and listen to the radio and try to play the songs. I began to rearrange hymns. Playing the piano was my getaway!

I finally got the courage to ask my father, who is a Pastor, to play for the church. He told me yes. So I started with the youth choir. It went very well. Then, the word got around that I was playing the piano.

One of my father's friends asked if could I play for their church. When my Dad shared this request with me, I was so excited. Then my Dad said, *"Calm down because this is serious."* His tone shook me. He went on to say, *"Dee Dee, you have a gift from God and you must never forget that."* I replied, *"Yes sir."* Then he said, *"God gave you this gift freely, so I better not hear of you charging for it, do you understand?"* I quickly responded, *"Yes sir."*

After I began to play for my Father's friend, the word about me playing began to travel around to other ministries and churches. More churches begin asking for me to come to play at their services and programs. However, I kept hearing my father's advice in my head. He always taught me that humility was the way to serve God.

God truly blessed me, people were very kind to me, and I was always grateful. As I grew up, I accepted my call into the ministry.

I tried to take the same principles taught by my father as I stepped into the preaching side of ministry. It was rough at first because people judge you by their requirements for an acceptable minister. I was rejected by two pastors of churches . The reasons they gave were legitimate, but I wasn't about to be their concubine just to get licensed. These men were very careful with their wording but careless with their gestures.

Somehow, I ended up in a situation where I wasn't only a musician. I was an accountant, liturgical dance leader, and the personal assistant to a couple in ministry. They eventually moved me into their home. I was cooking, cleaning, and babysitting. I truly loved this family and would do anything to help. The leader of the home, the pastor in which I was serving at the time, would pull me into his office and ask me how was my flesh? I was like huh? He told me I was a young and beautiful woman; and he was sure I had "needs".

I assured my pastor I was fine and that my flesh was under subjection. I was beginning to feel uncomfortable. I did a lot in this ministry, as a matter of fact, I never got to preach. I was only good for cooking, cleaning, administrative duties, babysitting and serving the First Lady. It was very frustrating but because I didn't have a place to stay and no income, I felt as though I was trapped. I was raised to respect my elders so I didn't talk back, challenge, or show disrespect. However, I'm seeing my humility slowly turning into humiliation.

I met a guy, we became friends and he wanted to date me. We would talk for hours on the phone and he would even come by the church to show me some chords on the organ. One night, I wrote him a letter and misted my favorite perfume on it. The next morning I knew I had to drop the church bills off at the post office so I'd figured I'd send my letter as well. The pastor decided to drop me off at the church and take the mail himself.

A few days went by and I noticed my friend never mentioned the letter. So I finally asked about it and found out that he never received it. I asked the pastor about it and he claimed he sent it off. In my gut, I knew he was lying. Two days later, my friend got my letter but the pages were out of order. I could not believe this dude read my letter to my friend! Next thing I know I'm in the office again being questioned about my flesh. I was also scolded for sending a perfumed letter to a man. I was livid and felt violated. Needless to say, I got out of there.

My humility has been constantly mishandled. When you have integrity predators, pharaohs, and pulpit pimps take advantage of you! Sometimes you feel your gift to serve is a curse because of the way people handle you.

A mindset of humility is present when you accept assignments to go on the road to preach and you do not charge those organizations as you could. On average, Apostles are blessed for their services at about $1200 to $1800 per assignment, but I'd never charged at that rate. However, the minimal fee that I ask is to cover the travel expenses and sometimes that ask is not met, even after being agreed upon.

Operating on the honor system can cause you to get burned or taken advantage of because the humble mindset is taken for granted. Of course, the ministry is not about the money, however, the Bible declares a workman is worthy of his hire. I kept my mouth shut and continued to serve regardless.

Humility is what God requires, but what happens when it turns into humiliation? When you look at Jesus' life He was very humble and went through humiliating things. Can you imagine being mocked, spat on, and falsely accused by the people you came to help? Of course, you can, we do it every day. The anointing on our lives is not a bubble to keep us safe, it's an oil to save others. When you are obedient to God it will cause attacks, ridicule, and abandonment from those you hold dear. Just because we obey God doesn't mean we are exempt from terrible treatment by humans. We have to be careful about the spirit of entitlement.

I went on an assignment to minister. The ministry that invited me treated me very well. Usually, when I'm on itinerate ministry I have to get contractual agreements signed to ensure coverage of expenses. However, this assignment didn't require that because of the integrity of the ministry.

Shortly after, I had another assignment where there was a contractual agreement. I poured out with intensity and completed with obedience to the Lord. They handed me an envelope before I left, and I placed it in my purse. When I got home it was not what we agreed upon. I was very upset. I felt like I won't take another assignment in that particular circle again! Especially after I had just been treated so well by strangers.

The Lord rebuked me. He reminded me that I had been several places where churches were unfair to me, but I was grateful for what they did give. I tithed and He blessed me. He

COMPILED BY DR. J. LE'RAY

reminded me of what my Father told me over 30 years ago. This gift came from God you don't have a right to put a price on it.

You see, just that quick that feeling of entitlement jumped on me. God had to remind me that my humility and gratitude has brought me as far as I have come in life period. So, never think your humility is a curse. Sometimes, when people know you are humble they will try to take advantage of it; however, God sees all. Know that there will be times you'll be treated well and at other moments not so much, but the saving grace is that God's grace is sufficient. Stay humble at all costs!

To be humiliated because I'm known for being a humble servant is an honor. It actually identifies me with Christ.

2 Timothy 2:11-13 *declares:*

It is a faithful saying: For if we be dead with him, we shall also live with him: If we suffer, we shall also reign with him: if we deny him, he also will deny us: If we believe not, yet he abideth faithful: he cannot deny himself.

1 Peter 5:6 declares:

Humble yourselves therefore under the mighty hand of God, that he may exalt you in due time:

It was humility that brought me into that great effectual door and it will be humility that will keep me there. That is the honor in humility, it's never about how you're treated only about how you respond. God's grace is sufficient.

INTERNAL REFLECTION QUESTIONS:

Do you love what you do enough to deny yourself of your fleshly desires?

_____

_____

_____

_____

_____

Are you willing to take a hit so someone else can grow without the warfare?

_____

_____

_____

_____

_____

Can you see the value of your life even in humiliating situations?

_____

_____

_____

_____

Power of Truth

By: *Patsy Clowney Bloom & Verganell Thomas Craig*

Truth is: conformity to fact or actuality; faithfulness to an original or to a standard. Truth is one powerful and perspective shifting word. It is a noun and a verb. Truth as a noun means in accordance with fact or reality, accurate or exact, and loyal or faithful. Truth as a verb means the quality or state of being true.

Truth is also a quality used to describe utterances that are from the Lord. As we journey, understanding what truth is and how it manifests in our life from our inner most being is critical. The devil is devoid of truth. In the Old and New Testaments, truth is a fundamental moral and personal quality of God.

It is proclaimed that God is "merciful and gracious, long suffering, and abounding in goodness and truth." He is a "God of truth without injustice". Furthermore, all of his paths are in "mercy and truth." All of God's works, percepts, and judgements are done in righteousness and truth. He promises his disciples that he would send *the spirit of truth: God is truth; the Spirit is truth; and Jesus is truth. Jesus said, "I am the way, the truth, and the life. No one comes to the father except through me"*

Jesus and the revelation of the spirit of truth, given through his apostles, are the final, ultimate revelation and definition of truth about God people, redemption, history and the world. "The law was given through Moses, but grace and truth came through Jesus Christ. Being open to seek truth, receive it, process it and apply it intertwined with application accelerates our ascension process.

SCRIPTURE REFERENCES

James 1:18, John 14:17-18, Psalms 25:5

WRITE THE VISION: MAKE IT PLAIN

Dr. Natalie Holts Davis

ifty years seems like a long time to push and fight for greater, and yet I stand poised, ready, and determined to push, fight, and pray for at least fifty more if it is God's will. My physical life began in 1969 at Hugh Spalding Hospital in Atlanta, GA. I was born and reared as the oldest of three children to loving, hardworking parents. My mother was an operations manager for Sun Trust bank and my father was a military airman turned yard foreman with Norfolk Southern railway. This was his "pay the bills" job. You see, my father was also a full-time AME pastor. Nathaniel Holts is a proud man, and during my childhood, he was determined not to need the church to support his family. I guess that's where I get my strong-willed determination from. A determined preacher's kid, with fifty years of truth to share. Imagine that.

A significant part of my two scores and ten have been journaling. For a lifetime, I've enjoyed putting pen to paper and making words summarize the reality that I experience every day. As a young "YPDer" (a member of the Young People's Division) in the AME church, I accepted the Lord, Jesus as my personal savior at the tender age of 9. This is significant because this is about the time we truly started going to church as a family on a regular basis. This was a time post parent separation, almost turned divorce, that my family began to truly operate as a unit; banned together in love, learning how to lean on Jesus and each other.

During this time, through Children's Church and under the leadership and direction of awesome ministry leaders, I was taught how to pray. **PRAY** – **P**raise, **R**epent, **A**sk, **Y**ield was a lesson drilled into me constantly in my early years. Using the Lord's prayer as a model and capitalizing on this acronym, not only was I taught how to pray, I was also encouraged to pray all the time and under any and every circumstance (I Thessalonians 5:17).

I was challenged as a child to write out my prayers and document the manifested effect of what I "asked" the Lord about and for each day. "Keep a record of just how good God has been and is being to you," echoed from every ministry leader. The result has been years of devotion and quiet time captured in printed or typed text in both tangible and, as of late, electronic journals. Not to mention, my Bible is one big journal of my spiritual study and just everyday life events. I often open up my Bible and make notes in the margins. My Bible is full of dated sermon titles and meaningful sermon notes scribbled beside the inspired scripture text. I know this would drive some crazy but for me, any revelation I get when reading or hearing the Word, I don't mind highlighting, underlining, sticky noting, or writing in the margins and blank spaces in my Bible to capture the essence of learned information, marked and notated for future reference.

Write the vision and make it plain on tablets, that he may run who reads it. For the vision is yet for an appointed time; But at the end it will speak, and it will not lie. Though it tarries, wait for it; Because it will surely come, It will not tarry. - **Habakkuk 2:2-3**

In other words, it bears witness to and "is" the truth. Considering the concept of truth, I want to share a couple of significantly connected entries in my life's journal that make me continue communicating my faith through written words. Constantly running this race with endurance, through faith, all while understanding that God's timing is perfect.

In December of 2010, my then pastor, the late Bishop Eddie Lee Long of New Birth Missionary Baptist Church asked us to write a letter to ourselves outlining resolutions and intended goals/visions for the coming year. We were to bring those letters to the altar during Watch Night (New Year's Eve) service in a self-addressed stamped envelope.

It was communicated to the congregation that a group of ministry leaders would pray over the letters for six months and then, later that year, mail them back to us during late spring/early summer around June. The purpose of this was to document the progress of our goals and prayers over the half year period.

At the time, I started the letter with a very specific prayer for myself and my family. I then wrote out goals for each area of my life that I wanted God to deal with and change for the better - my family, my finances, my faith, my personal development, and lastly, my occupation. Filtering my testimony through the Habakkuk scripture, I want to share my truth.

Let's start with my goals and vision for personal development. The first goal bulleted in this category was *"Let me realize my dream of being Dr. Natalie Davis soon."* At that time, the Lord had blessed me to have obtained my bachelor's in Business Administration, my teaching credentials for grades K-8, a master's in School Administration, and a Specialist's degree in Educational

Leadership. I had finished my Specialist degree in May of 2006 with the full intention to have my Doctorate completed no later than 2008 (two years later).

In their hearts humans plan their course, but the LORD establishes their steps. **- Proverbs 16:9, NIV**

Surprise, soon after graduating in May of 2006, I found out that I was pregnant and had my youngest son, Caleb Theron Davis later that year. I might add that he is indeed a living, breathing, walking miracle. You see, I carried Caleb full term with no complications, at age 38 with three-fourths of my cervix removed. Four years before Caleb, I was blessed to bore my first son, Cameron Tyrell, and after this pregnancy, my cervix was taken because of precancerous activity. I was told that I would not be able to have and/or carry any more children. Of course, our amazing God saw fit to give us a Christmas surprise through Davis child number four affectionately known as our Flourishing Finish!

Fast forward four years later to December 2010 and back to my bulleted goal on the letter I was writing. Believe me, my aspirations of my doctorate degree was a huge goal that I truly wanted to check off my list. In my mind and heart, I was clearly off schedule by quite a few years.

He said to them: "It is not for you to know the times or dates the Father has set by his own authority. **Acts 1:7, NIV**

One of the keywords in my goal was "soon". However, I am a living witness that our timing is not always God's timing. As I wrote the goal, instead of just enjoying the journey, I was truly getting impatient. Although I wrote this goal entering 2011, it was not until two years later in 2013 that I was successful in pursuing this purpose driven goal further.

After returning in an instructional leadership role, to a school where I'd previously been a teacher in January of 2013, I decided to go back to the university where I completed my Specialist's degree. Not knowing how I would pay for it, because part of the reason that I was not able to continue school in the first place, was that I'd exhausted all my financial aid, I asked the school about my options.

After evaluating my transcript, I was told that if I didn't enroll before the fall semester of that year, I would have to start over from scratch in the new doctoral program. None of my course work post Specialist's degree would count. Based on the timing of my last course work, I was one semester away from not being able to continue in the program I started after my Specialist's. Not to mention that the school was combining my current program together with another to add more to the required coursework. I quickly enrolled in the summer semester, out of pocket, and prayed *"Lord, let your will be done."*

I tell you the truth, if you have faith as small as a mustard seed, you can say to this mountain, 'Move from here to there' and it will move. Nothing will be impossible for you. **Matthew 17:20, NIV**

Through negotiating with the school, and many prayers, I was able to return to school and secure funding for that semester as well as for the balance of my education. I thought that all was well with the world. I was able to get back to school, and I had managed to beat the deadline that would require me to start and complete a whole new doctoral program. I was able to pay for starting costs and get financial aid to cover the rest.

I was pursuing my goal identified in 2011, and then a

roadblock.   In 2014 my maternal grandmother died. My grandmother was my truest friend and dearest confidant. This blow was significant because my grandmother was my biggest cheerleader and a true motivation for continuing. When she died, I had to continue to reference THE letter so that I would continue to run with it and my goal would continue being realized.

Seeing my goal made the idea more real and, because of her death, I wanted to complete my degree more than ever. Before she died, she would tell everyone, "my grandbaby is a doctor!" This continued to happen even after she was corrected several times, so to me, remembering those proud Grandmamma moments made me that much more determined to make it true.

With support from my amazing husband, who fed children, helped with the cooking, did the cleaning, assisted with extra activities for the children, and did anything else that helped me to focus on the goal, my written vision became a reality. On May 7, 2015, I defended my dissertation research and heard the words, *"Well done, Dr. Natalie Davis! Your defense was a success."*

The celebration and conferring of my degree took place on December 5, and my truest friend was with me. I marched down the aisle with joy in my heart and a picture of Ruth T. Williams (my grandmother) in my bosom. The vision is yet for an APPOINTED time. It shall speak and shall not lie. (Habakkuk 2:3)

Now thanks be unto God, which always causeth us to triumph in Christ - **II Corinthians 2:14, NKJV**

Another written truth that came to fruition from my written goals outlined in THE letter is my current career. My ultimate dream job and vision for myself was to become a principal. However, in writing my goals down, I decided not to limit God. The prayer in my letter asked God to give me the job of His choice, and He did just that.

On February 23, 2018, at noon, my principal called me into his office and shared some news that would change the course of my career. I knew that what he proposed would not be in my best interest, so I communicated my intention to explore other options. Had it not been for that conversation, I probably would have been content with just settling with where I was.

I had seen my degree vision come to pass, and many failed attempts at upward movement in school-based leadership made me wonder if God was just saying be still. I might also add, up until this point, every career decision I'd ever made had been with my family, specifically my children in mind. Though I wanted to be a school principal, I wouldn't just apply for or accept anything that came along. I was very intentional with my application choices, but they never seemed to be the right fit.

Through divine connections and relationships, he granted me my dream job. God did exceedingly and abundantly above what I could ever ask or think (Ephesians 3:20). At the right time, He reminded me that delay is not denial. All the administrative positions I had applied for in the past, paled in comparison to my current career reality. As a Federal Programs Coordinator, I am living my best life! But I do so knowing that through God's guidance and grace, greater is still yet to come.

INTERNAL REFLECTION QUESTIONS:

What truths have you written plainly for yourself and/or others to see that have come to pass?

_____

_____

_____

_____

_____

What truths about God's word have been illuminated for you after reading this passage?

_____

_____

_____

_____

_____

What behaviors in your own life will change as a result of having read this passage?

_____

_____

_____

_____

_____

ROOTED AND BUILT UP IN HIM

By: Erica M. Daniel

Search me, O God, and know my heart; test me and know my anxious thoughts. Point out anything in me that offends you, and lead me along the path of everlasting life. - **Psalms 139: 23-24 NLT**

For the first time in a long time, I met someone, and the connection was undeniable. Unsure of how to proceed, I pushed back thinking I was not ready for a relationship. Over time, our connection grew and we both knew we could no longer suppress our feelings towards one another. That was it! We were to move forward with our love story.

Very early on we knew we needed God to be in our midst for the relationship to sustain. Not only did we support one another, but we also prayed together as often as we could. Our prayer for our relationship was simple, *"God reveal to us if we are meant to be with one another."* My heart grew fonder and fonder with every day that passed. While we agreed to wait for God's confirmation, our discussion on marriage and allowing our families to meet became a common area of excitement.

This was it! I found my Boaz!

Truth Hurts

Something's off.

I sensed it.

While we still prayed and laughed, I knew something just wasn't right. I couldn't place my finger on it and assumed there was an issue with work, thus prompting this change and distance.

And then 'it' happened.

He broke up with me. Not because I lacked. Not because I did not make his cup full. Not because I was not beautiful, established or kind enough but because *she* made his cup overflow. *She* being a close friend, my sister, my advocate, my rock, and my support system.

My heart, once a precious stone held in high esteem and admiration, was shattered, the pieces so small it felt beyond repair. Valueless. Engulfed in despair and anger I suffocated in my sorrow and sadness. I drowned in silence trying to shield the actions of my sister-friend and love. Even with witnessing the daily disdain and piercing eyes of pure hatred I tried to remain loyal and unwavering.

I wept.

For weeks I held all of my emotions inside afraid that expressing my truths would hinder their growth and the new relationship. I danced through the motions of life, while slowly dying on the inside. Often, I sat in the dark, alone, fearful and scared to venture beyond my home; believing my presence would somehow bring shame and disgrace to the new couple. The truth is, I felt compelled to protect them, to allow them to have their chance to be judgment free.

Imagine, there I was broken, afraid, and trapped in a self-induced prison created by my mind. Day after day, the new couple mocked me. They ridiculed me with their growing love for one another and hate towards me. On many occasions, they attacked my character making public untruthful claims to those they knew were close to me. They would encourage their audience to find me weak, unfit, untruthful and unreliable. As each day went by, and as each call came in, I went deeper and deeper into the sunken place of despair, pity, and heartache. Emotionally incapacitated, spiritually attacked, and physically weak.

You intended to harm me, but God intended it all for good. He brought me to this position so I could save the lives of many people.   Genesis 50:20

But God.

Too often when seeking the truth, we do not turn to God, we turn to the world and the people within it. We trust the opinions of others before even consulting God. During this time of heartache, I found refuge in my dark place, my solitude. I would ask people hypothetical questions, trying to grasp onto some form of hope for my future. I'd hide from my offenders in the presence of those whom I knew were spiritually strong. Yet, the truth of it all had not hit me at that point.

Peace I leave with you; my peace I give you. I do not give to you as the world gives. Do not let your hearts be troubled and do not be afraid. - **John 14:27**

You see unlike people, God's word never changes. His truths and his promises remain and will be honored when you chose to fully rely on him. The truth is, through this entire travesty and time of devastation, God was standing by my side. In fact, one of the many truths found in the Word, Joshua 1:5 states, *"**No** one will be able to stand against you as long as you live. For I will be with you as I was with Moses. I will not fail you or abandon you."*

When I turned my eyes from the people around me and diverted my attention from the pain placed upon me and offered everything to God, he embraced me in his warmth. He used his Word to remind me of his truths and his promises. Joshua 1:9 clearly says, *"Have I not commanded you? Be strong and courageous. Do not be afraid; do not be discouraged, for the Lord your God will be with you wherever you go."*

Slowly, I began to turn over all of my thoughts of worry, failure, and inferiority to God. I began to trust my process by acknowledging the power of God as it is stated in his word. Philippians 4:6-7 says, *"**6** Do not be anxious about anything, but in every situation, by prayer and petition, with thanksgiving, present your requests to God. **7** And the peace of God, which transcends all understanding, will guard your hearts and your minds in Christ Jesus."*

Every day I turned all of my anxious thoughts to Christ. I followed the *Lord's Prayer* (Matthew 6:9-13) and prayed for those who trespassed against me. I prayed for them to find peace. I prayed for God to do mighty works in their life. I prayed for their businesses to be expanded. I prayed for forgiveness, peace, understanding and for the fruit of the spirit (Galatians 5:22-23) to grow from within me. I rooted myself in Godly principles.

13 Brothers and sisters, I do not consider myself yet to have taken hold of it. But one thing I do: Forgetting what is behind and straining toward what is ahead, 14 I press on toward the goal to win the prize for which God has called me heavenward in Christ Jesus. - **Philippians 3:13-14**

I continued to explore God's truth and prayed over my mind

and my heart. I demanded it to be turned back over to the Lord. I began to command my thoughts to be obedient to Christ, 2 Corinthians 10:5, *"We demolish arguments and every pretension that sets itself up against the knowledge of God, and we take captive every thought to make it obedient to Christ"* and I stood, *"rooted and built up in him, strengthened in the faith as you were taught, and overflowing with thankfulness,"* Colossians 2:7.

Stand firm in God's TRUTH.

Matthew 6: 25-34 eloquently instructs us not to worry and to know our Heavenly Father already knows our needs.

25 "That is why I tell you not to worry about everyday life—whether you have enough food and drink, or enough clothes to wear. Isn't life more than food, and your body more than clothing? 26 Look at the birds. They don't plant or harvest or store food in barns, for your heavenly Father feeds them. And aren't you far more valuable to him than they are? 27 Can all your worries add a single moment to your life? 28 "And why worry about your clothing? Look at the lilies of the field and how they grow. They don't work or make their clothing, 29 yet Solomon in all his glory was not dressed as beautifully as they are. 30 And if God cares so wonderfully for wildflowers that are here today and thrown into the fire tomorrow, he will certainly care for you. Why do you have so little faith? 31 "So don't worry about these things, saying, 'What will we eat? What will we drink? What will we wear?' 32 These things dominate the thoughts of unbelievers, but your heavenly Father already knows all your needs. 33 Seek the Kingdom of God above all else, and live righteously, and he will give you everything you need. 34 "So don't worry about tomorrow, for tomorrow will bring its own worries. Today's trouble is enough for today.

There is power in the Word of God. Jeremiah 29: 11 says, *"For I know the plans I have for you,"* declares the Lord, *"plans to prosper you and not to harm you, plans to give you hope and a future."* In order to feel the fullness of God and to see all He has in store for your life, you must stand firm in the Word of God. It is the Word that is our truth. The power of the word cannot be denied. The power of the Word fights battles the human mind is unable to conceptualize (2 Corinthians 10:3-5). The power of the Word is our TRUTH. When you believe it (Matthew 21:22), you will soar and fulfill your divine purpose (Isaiah 40:31). You are called by God to do great things (Isaiah 43).

Remember God's Word will never fail you. In fact, it is a *lamp for my feet, a light on my path*, Psalm 119:105. The truth is, it may hurt today, but God uses all opportunities to be glorified. Rest assured, even in your pain, God is in control.

May this truth set you free from the bondage and into his secret place.

INTERNAL REFLECTION QUESTIONS:

What truths are you placing your faith in? Are they spiritually sound and rooted in the principles of God?

_____

_____

_____

_____

_____

What truths have God revealed to you?

_____

_____

_____

_____

_____

What three things can you begin to do today to allow God's Truth to guide you and rest upon your heart?

_____

_____

_____

_____

_____

TRIUMPHANTLY BROKEN

By: Temika Powers

*H*ave you ever felt, or maybe still feel, you were nonexistent? Do you ever feel like you are here but not really here? Yeah, that was exactly how I've felt from childhood all the way to adulthood. I felt I was in a place I did not belong. I felt like my life was not real and it was all a dream.

I was birthed into an environment that was not conducive to my growth. For a long time, I walked around feeling unloved and never good enough. It seemed as though I was always in situations that kept me in the mindset of never measuring up, never being accepted for me, and always having to give or do in order to be apart.

Throughout life, I found myself in cycles of rejection. I had begun to believe that was how it was supposed to be due to how my environment presented it to me time and time again. I had one parent that was in the home but not really of the home. I never heard I love you, was shown that I was loved, told I did a good job, or was even told the words, *"proud of you"* growing up.

Then there was another parent who had other daughters but never came back for me. All I could think of as a child is, *"why am I not good enough to be loved by the ones who made me?"* Then, I found myself looking for love and acceptance in other people rather than loving and accepting myself.

How could I? I was never taught or shown how that would look. My environment taught me to look to other people to validate me and show me my worth. I ended up getting pregnant at the age of seventeen and leaving home to be with someone who was in lust with me, not in love with me. Again, I was in another cycle of rejection, not feeling loved, valuable, or even accepted.

However, I remained in that situation for years because of fear. I feared I would have to go back home. I feared I would fail as a mother. I feared I would struggle to a greater degree; not with just one child now, but with two children to raise. I feared my children would lack and suffer as I did as a child. All in fear, I knew I did not want my children to experience the hardships and difficulties I did growing up.

Since I had a mindset of rejection, I started to accept not being loved and valued. I did not value myself. I started to believe that I always had to say "yes" to people so that they would want to be around me. I began to believe my environment, and that maybe that was how it was supposed to be. I was here but not present.

Things continued to spiral downwards for me and my family after my nine-year-old daughter, at the time, wanted to have a talk with me. She asked if we could go in the room behind the closed bedroom door where she revealed to me that she had been molested by someone she called "papa". This was someone we all trusted and had grown to love.

I could not believe this had happened to my baby. The main

people, my children, whom I was trying to cover and protect, to the best of my ability, have now experienced rejection, dysfunction, and confusion. I never thought that you could instantly go from loving a person to hating them, but I did.

I wanted revenge and I wanted it done my way. All I could ask was, *"why God?"* Not long after we found out that my daughter had been molested, I found out that I had been cheated on multiple times. The crazy thing is, I had already, in my mind, given him a pass to cheat because somehow I knew that he would do so.

My thoughts were that he would cheat with a random chick I did not know and that would be the thing that would help me deal with it even better. I was so wrong on so many levels. The cheating happened but happened with females that I knew and was extremely close to. When all of these things came to light, I was devastated. I immediately knew what anxiety attacks were and they became frequent, on a daily basis, two to three times if not more.

I became disturbingly depressed. No matter how hard I tried to do life, life was kicking my tail. It really was one thing after the other. I was being brutally beat down by life. I tried to pray, but I could never finish the prayer. I tried to read the Bible, and even quote scriptures, but I had no relief.

I even continued to preach and teach the Word while harboring hate and rage in my heart. The more I thought about my situations throughout my life, the worse I became in my depression. I was not only a mother, wife, sister, daughter, but I was a minister. How could this be? A minister of the Gospel of Jesus Christ and I was going through all this heartache and pain.

I was being tormented by the thoughts of my daughter being molested. I was being tortured by the thoughts of being faithful to an unfaithful person. I was being taunted by the thoughts of never being good enough and never being worthy enough to be truly loved and appreciated for just being me. When I called on God, I felt nothing changed but that was only because I chose to be filled with anger and carry an unforgiving heart.

Why was God not answering me? Why was God not raining down hell's fire on these individuals that hurt me and hurt my children? Why God, why? Within myself, I had a right to be angry. I had a right to want revenge. I had a right to destroy the lives of those who came for me and mine. I had a right! But God, why are you not as angry with these people as I am? You are the One who can really do something about it, and that would make my life so much better.

Those prayers were not being answered and I began to resent God. I did not want any dealings with God because I felt He didn't have my back like I thought He should. My perception of life and love had been altered tremendously by the way my environment was and by my thinking. I began to have an altered perception of God. I thought there was no way a God so big, mighty, and all-powerful had me be born into chaos and dysfunction; and then allowed me to go through life the way I did and not do something drastic about it.

I pulled back from God and began to live life the way I wanted. I started drinking heavily to drown out the voices, to medicate the hurt. I even thought that I was getting back at God. I was so wrong! I ended up making things worse for myself. But at the time, I didn't think so and somehow I felt justified for why I was behaving the way I was.

You know… growing up, I had always heard how there are three sides to every story - your side, their side, and the truth. Well, when I told "my side" I was right, and it was the truth. I was the victim and everyone else was wrong. You know, it is so easy to point the finger at others because then you feel you don't have to be held accountable.

The truth is, I did not have to give into and accept the situations and circumstances that were created. Truth is, I could have made the right choices to be able to obtain what I really wanted for my life. Truth is, I did not have to repeat the vicious cycles of what society and my environment told me I was going to be and do. Truth is, God loved me still, and He always showed me ways to have better and do better, but I did not take heed to the signs.

I found myself in a place where I was completely broken. I was in a place where I was so empty and so alone. No matter how many parties I threw and how many people were around, I felt that I was the only one there. I was just an empty shell of a person. I was in a deep dark hole and I could not climb out.

There was no light in sight. My children came to me and said *"Mom, what's wrong? You're smiling but what is wrong?"* They went on to say, *"whatever it is, we just want you to be happy."* At that moment, there was a pinhole of light. I kept repeating it over and over to myself what I heard my children say *"we just want you to be happy."* I released a scream and began to weep, all I could do was call on and cry out to God for help and mercy. I told God that I didn't want to just be here, but I want to be present and deal with the absolute truth.

I had to be real with myself and God, and I told God that I

didn't want to be suicidal anymore. I wanted to be a great mother to my children. I told God that I surrender to His will for my life and if He would just give me peace and restore my life that I would pour out all He has poured into me, no matter what.

But I knew I had to forgive in a major way, and truthfully forgive others, myself, and God. I needed to be free and I mean free for real. God heard me and He answered. I was healed, delivered, and set free. God restored, renewed, and also blessed me with the love of my life!

Truth is, God is a healer and a restorer. In order to truly be healed and delivered you have to face the absolute truth and deal with the root issues. This way you can experience and walk in absolute freedom and true genuine love.

INTERNAL REFLECTION QUESTIONS:

Are we willing and ready to accept that we have been broken in some areas; and that we need the power and love of God to heal us completely?

_____

_____

_____

_____

_____

Can you love you in the areas of your life that may seem less valuable, less desirable, and not good enough?

_____

_____

_____

_____

_____

I challenge each of us to identify those areas of weakness in your life and love on them. List at least 3 areas in which you will begin to nurture.

_____

_____

_____

_____

_____

Power of Discipline

By: Patsy Clowney Bloom & Verganell Thomas Craig

The goal of discipline is to teach obedience. Discipline can be viewed as how parents discipline their children, how authorities discipline those under their authority, how Abba Father disciplines His children, and how we discipline ourselves.

Either way, discipline is the practice of training people to obey rules or a code of behavior, often using punishment to correct disobedience. This means that when we are undisciplined or lack self-control, the result is consequences yielding lessons learned. Discipline transforms our lifestyle through consistent choices of obedience.

The biblical concept of discipline has both a positive side (instructions, knowledge and training) and a negative aspect (correction, punishment, and reproof). Those who refuse to submit to God's positive discipline by obeying his laws will experience God's negative discipline through his wrath and judgement.

Disciples were taught by God for the purpose of education, instruction, and training, corrective guidance and discipline. As written in Proverbs 3:11, we are reminded to "despise not the discipline of the Lord, nor faint when we are rebuked of Him. For whom the Lord loves He disciplines."

SCRIPTURE REFERENCES

Revelations 3:19, Proverb 6:23, Hebrew 12:5-11

THE DISCIPLINED DEATH

By: Alicia D. Foust

rowing up my life was very peculiar. God blessed me to grow up with a family; parents, siblings, and my grandmother under one roof. Most people would think that was the best life, but for me, it was the beginning of my death walk. I was very demanding and confrontational, and it kept me in trouble.

What no one knew was I would have dreams and visions of myself doing grown-up things yet trapped in the body of a little girl. I would have dreams of things and then all of a sudden, I would see things on the news just as it was in my dreams. These events frightened me because I felt responsible for them happening; but who would believe a little girl?

In my dreams, I would feel so empowered. So, when I was awake and was asked to do something, I would ask why. Of course, this was considered disrespectful and would result in disciplinary action. Something would come over me and I would be very sorrowful and apologetic. However, it wasn't valid in their eyes because I kept doing the same things repeatedly. I really didn't mean to be disrespectful. I couldn't explain how I felt like Superwoman, but I was expected to carry myself like Strawberry Shortcake.

Being in school was similar and at times worse. I was very intelligent, a straight "A" student. However, that caused the popular girls in school to tease me. My parents dressed me well and my hair was always done so I was viewed as "bougie". I was looking desperately for acceptance, so I became a class clown, stopped answering questions, turned homework in late, and even offered my snack money just to gain friendship and acceptance. Only to still be rejected by my classmates and ejected from the classrooms. To add to it all, my new behavior got me in trouble at home. Discipline, in my mind, had become rejection so I was at a loss of who to be. I would sit in my room and cry for hours, just wondering if I would ever have a normal life.

Being an asthmatic child, I wasn't allowed to go out and play like my brothers. So, I spent a lot of time with my grandmother. She is the reason I am very domesticated. I was always at peace around her. She understood me more than anyone, although not fully.

95% of my time at home I was in my room alone. I'd write songs, sermons, and love letters. I would get the hymn book and figure out ways to rearrange them. I began playing the piano and it seems as if that would be the only time, I could get my daddy to smile. I was dedicated to my lessons and would listen to the radio to tried to learn the latest gospel songs by ear. I ended up playing for church and it seemed that was the only time I could gain any type of affirmation. This was the beginning of using ministry as a hiding place. I was instructed by my father that my playing was a gift from God, and I was not to charge people; whatever they give me, I was to accept it gratefully. How could this gift be accepted, and I was still afraid to talk about my other gift?

Discipline is defined in Merriam- Webster's Dictionary as, "control gained by enforcing obedience or order, punishment or training that corrects, molds, or perfects the mental faculties or moral character." Death is defined as, "a permanent cessation of all vital functions, the end of life, or beyond endurance." I am sure by now one might wonder how these two words connect. What I have discovered is this is the only way to describe my life. It's been a disciplined death.

Although parts of me were being suppressed, due to my low self-esteem, many parts were being awakened that were critical to my destiny. Discipline is a word that is shunned nowadays. We live in a society where if you discipline your own offspring the authorities can be called in to interfere with the course a parent has implemented. Nowadays, if discipline is implemented in church, you're accused of being judgmental; when the plan is to keep souls from being judged when the Lord returns. This has truly affected the power of the mind. Daily people are making short-sighted decisions because no one is casting vision, just inciting division.

I have found that my life was a disciplined death. It wasn't that I was lacking affirmation. God was teaching me not to be caught up in the approval of others. God knew the path I was taking, there would be very little pats on the back and well wishes. I was being conditioned to die to my flesh, also known as feelings. What I was being called to was greater than I could imagine so I couldn't stay there without this type of discipline.

If you're going to impact people you must be able to endure impacts from attacks. There are people that plot people's demise, they are influenced by Satan. In order to counterattack the plot, there's conditioning needed. It is imperative that I die daily in

order to execute my assignment. As a child, I would take blows but keep moving.

Once I became an adult and was fully aware of my gifts and callings. My resilience however, was not as strong. The power of my mind was being attacked. The enemy was screaming in my ear and emotions drowning out the still small voice of God. This is why peace is so critical to our lives. When one is not at peace it affects your thoughts, health, and even your wealth. Romans 12:2 states, *"And be not conformed to this world: but be ye transformed by the renewing of your mind, that ye may be able to prove what is that good, and acceptable, and perfect will of God."* Philippians 4:7 states *"And the peace of God, which passeth all understanding, shall keep your hearts and minds through Christ Jesus."* With that being said, it is imperative that you guard your mind. My grandmother always told me that an idle mind was the devil's workshop. The mind is so powerful! Whatever you think, you become.

I understand why my life has been the way it is. In order for me to be a disciple of Jesus Christ, I had to be disciplined. Corrected to change. Chastised to develop character. Exposed so I could be elevated. Disappointed so I could be a deliverer. Wounded so I could administer healing. My death these last 16,276 days was disciplined. Although I couldn't understand the isolation, the rejection, the lack of affirmation at the times I experienced it I see it was for my making.

Many times, what we count as a loss is a major gain. Psalm 37:23 states *"The steps of a good man are ordered by the Lord: and he delighted in his way."* Discipline is not really punishment but preparation. The temporary pain or discomfort is nothing compared to the blessings on the other side. If you're going to be successful at anything, discipline is a must. Your ways are not His ways and your thoughts are not His thoughts. So that is why death is necessary with discipline. John 12:24 states *"Verily, verily I say unto you, except a corn of wheat fall into the ground and die, it abideth alone: but if it die, it bringeth forth much fruit."*

The disciplined death is not about me or you, it's about those that God has entrusted to your care through the gifts on the inside of you. The enemy's job is to convince you that your life has no purpose or value so, go ahead and kill yourself. That, Beloved, is a reckless death. No one benefits from it but you, because it calmed your mental anguish. But the earth will groan and moan for you because, what you allowed to be buried inside of you is unavailable to those that God promised you were coming. We will never understand the mind of God, but if we follow what Prophet Isaiah penned in chapter 26 verse 3 which says, *"Thou wilt keep him in perfect peace, whose mind is stayed on thee: because he trusteth in thee."* At that point, we can fulfill purpose, destiny, and promise.

Every day I had to die so others may live. Only a life hid in Christ will truly understand. It's imperative that you let your light shine to lead others out of the darkness. You know the way, you are familiar with the journey, you are aware of the side effects. Let your life and your light be the prescription someone is looking for. This is the Power of A Renewed Mind!

INTERNAL REFLECTION QUESTIONS:

Do you want destiny bad enough?

_____

_____

_____
_____
_____

Are you willing to sacrifice everything except your authenticity?

_____
_____
_____
_____
_____

Do you now understand that your life is a process to the promise?

_____
_____
_____
_____
_____

STANDING ON HIS PROMISES

OUT, THROUGH, AND IN

By: Elle Dean

*I*t was the year 2000, I had been happily married for six years with two perfect children. Trey was one year old and Leah was three years old. This was my sixth year in this highly suburban school district.

I began as a high school assistant principal and a year later found myself promoted to an elementary principal position. The neighborhood was beautiful. The entrance adorned with a beautiful decorative brick wall. Across the street from the school was a pond filled with ducks and geese; so much so, we actually had "duck walking" warning traffic signs. This was a school with a representation of all ethnicities and economic backgrounds; inclusive of students who lived in federally assisted housing; and children from single parent and two-parent households.

The district designated the campus as a Title I elementary school, which meant I had the highest free and reduced student population of all elementary schools. Additionally, we had the Prekindergarten Program for Children with Disabilities (PPCD), the Autism unit, and the district Behavior Adjust Class. Needless to say, I had a potpourri of pupils!

The parent involvement at the campus was phenomenal! Student academic performance increased every year. This was my sixth year and everything on paper spoke success, but I felt I could do more. I felt I had more to give. I prayed to God, "*show me where I can be beneficial for your kingdom*". I wanted a position that benefitted me as a wife, mother, and a child of God.

As a principal, we were required to attend job fairs in the area to assist in recruiting and hiring teachers. I always looked forward to attending job fairs as I was likely to see old colleagues from across the Metroplex. Walking through the convention center hall, I heard my name called. I turned and saw a colleague from my former district. She shared that she had been promoted. I was excited for her because this was a return to a department which she was instrumental in developing. Her enthusiasm about the new position exuded through her eyes and in her voice as she described how she was forming a team. She said, "*why don't you come work for me.*" I laughed and said, "*you are kidding, right?*" At that moment, a teacher candidate approached inquiring about an open position, ending our conversation.

For the rest of the job fair, I pondered working for this phenomenal woman. She had a reputation of excellence and an astute knowledge of education. The thought of returning to the school district where I graduated high school, my mother still lived in the area, my son would attend Prekindergarten in the area, felt good and right. At the end of the job fair, I approached her and said, "*I'm interested; what are my next steps?*" She indicated I needed to complete the online application and call her once it's completed.

I shared the possibility of this new career adventure with my husband. I shared my positive thoughts around our son in school in the area and the opportunity to increase my knowledge and skill set. The new title would be 'specialist'. We prayed God would open this door if it was His will. I prayed that if this was my next step in serving God, that He moved me in the new position. We referred to Proverbs 3:1-6 that reminds us to *"trust in the Lord with All Your Heart"*.

The process of applying for the job was a time of soul searching. Matthew 6:34 says *"therefore do not be anxious about tomorrow, for tomorrow will be anxious for itself. Sufficient for the day is its own trouble."* It was my relationship with God that sustained me during this rigorous process. Ultimately, I was offered the job and my new journey was about to begin.

My joy of God working in my life was difficult to contain. I shared my happiness with my friends, coworkers, and family. But, the joy wasn't returned. I was taken aback when people didn't share my excitement. It was difficult to receive that some of the closest people to me didn't understand why I would change jobs and positions. I was hurt to my core. Staying focused on God's plan in spite of the opinions of others was a true test.

Working back in the large urban district was thrilling. One of the most rewarding was the opportunity to take my son to Prekindergarten daily for two years. We would stop at the donut shop, go through McDonald's, and Starbucks required a weekly visit. My new position also required me to assist in training 500 new teachers over the summer months. We were tasked with organizing the day, scheduling trainers, ensuring teachers signed in and out, and that instructional materials were on site. After the summer session training was complete, the focus was on the execution of the plan.

Initially, I was overwhelmed with the sheer numbers and magnitude of the work. Thankfully, God sent me colleagues that allowed me to learn as we completed the summer session. As a principal, you focus on your staff, students, and parents. In this new position, I had to think about preparing teachers to teach. I had a principal perspective, so I knew exactly what principals expected.

In the new position, I was assigned teacher interns in 33 schools! Wow! Talking about putting mileage on my vehicle! I loved reconnecting to the art of teaching. As an educator, the magic ends and begins with student academic success in the classroom experienced between the teacher and the student! Watching the novice teachers and coaching them brought unbelievable joy. They saw me as a coach instead of an evaluator. They understood my job was to assist, help, and grow them.

But just as life would have it, there were challenges with the job. The mileage on the family vehicle increased, which began to reflect in increased repairs. In addition, my talents were noticed so I was asked to take on special projects, including traveling monthly to recruit new teachers. I also accepted the assignment as the Higher Education Liaison, which involved coordinating university coursework for the 500+ teacher interns.

The Higher Ed partners represented nine universities in the Dallas/Fort Worth metroplex. In meeting with them I was overjoyed to reconnect with a former colleague who was now working with the university. After our meetings, we would catch up over a quick bite of lunch. Her support was pivotal as I worked with the typically male-dominated higher education representatives.

Along with my daily expectations, the additional assignments began to require more time away from family. My husband traveled two weeks out of the month, and now I was traveling once a month. It really taxed our children and our marriage. But I knew God planted me in this position for a reason. I prayed and asked God to speak to my discouragement. He quickly responded that I was on His time. I was directed to Numbers 23:19 *"God is not a man, that He should lie, Nor a son of man that He should repent; Has He said, and will He not do it? Or has He spoken, and will He not make it good?"*

Staying committed to the assignment, I flourished and during my second year, I was asked to take on a new role in the department. My undergraduate minor was Spanish, our director remembered that and asked that I join the bilingual team! Now my travel involved international recruiting, visas, culture and language. My professional skill set was being enhanced exponentially!

Working with the bilingual teacher candidates was eye-opening. We were literally changing lives and generations by offering teaching opportunities. But again, the joy in the career was a juxtaposition to my home life. Annually, we were recruiting, hiring and training over 300 bilingual teachers. Thankfully, I had a huge village support. My aunt kept my son daily until my husband or I got off work which was from 6:00 pm to 6:30 pm most days. Thankfully, my mom assisted with meals and would pick up my daughter as well. It took a team to coordinate our weekly routine.

In April 2003, I found myself close to completing the third year of my career assignment. My son was now preparing to transition from Prekindergarten to Kindergarten. He would return to our home school district to attend school with his sister. The thought of having both children in the same school warmed my heart. It would provide stability and consistency. The benefits of the transition of the upcoming school year were glaringly evident.

In speaking with a former colleague, she mentioned a position in our home school district. I immediately looked at the job description and the contact name. To my surprise, my former colleague, who was working in higher education, had returned to a school district. Namely, my home school district and was the hiring contact. I immediately contacted her, applied and after a rigorous interview process, I was named as the director of special programs. My years as the title I principal and my experience with bilingual education combined prepared me to be the ideal candidate for the position. Additionally, the "home field" advantage gave me the edge over other candidates. After working in the director position for one year, I was promoted to Assistant Superintendent!

My initial prayer, some three years ago, asking God to place me in a position that benefitted my children, me as a wife, and a child of God had come to fruition! I was able to work in the district with my children from kindergarten to graduation! I was blessed to witness their daily accomplishments, field trips, and programs. I was able to have lunch with them weekly.

My commitment to God's plan challenged me to be disciplined and live by faith. Yes, God had a plan, but you can't eat the fruit today off of the seed that you planted last week. Time is needed to cultivate the earth to allow the seed to go through the stages of growth. Three years of discipline, focus and consistency led to a now 15-year career explosion that only God could ordain. Just as God did with the children of Israel; God led them "through" the wilderness to test them and humble them to trust

God. After the test, God leads them out of the wilderness to the Promised Land demonstrating his promises fulfilled.

INTERNAL REFLECTION QUESTIONS:

Up to this point in your relationship with God, what have you understood "discipline" to mean in your Christian life?

_____

_____

_____

_____

_____

Share when you felt God challenged you to be disciplined. What circumstances in your life needed to be disciplined?

_____

_____

_____

_____

_____

What are some practical ways you kept your focus on staying disciplined? Share the results of your continued discipline.

_____

_____

_____

_____

_____

THE THREAD OF DISCIPLINE

By: Kenya Posey

As a mother, wife, full-time RN, and entrepreneur, life can get crazy and chaotic at times. Even after committing to being a co-author in this anthology I struggled with the decision of giving up and not moving forward to tell my story. Then, I prayed over the decision to continue in hopes that my story may impact someone else's life to not give up.

Life happens to everyone and whether you choose to move forward or stay where you are is a choice. And our choices can impact the big picture of our WHY. Our why is what drives our motivation. Your why should always be your inspiration. My why is, being able to spend more quality time with my family.

I have been wrestling with the decision for years to become my own boss. After putting in so many hours as an employee and being compensated, not by my work and skills; however, in some circumstances, by the company's budget, can be disappointing. I've always been that employee that strives to be the leader on my job and be the best at it.

However, my mindset was not built to stay in the same job for years. Albert Einstein said it best, *"The definition of insanity is doing the same thing over and over again, but expecting different results".*

Although I still currently continue to work full time as an RN, I know I am planting seeds to grow my future endeavors.

As I look back over my life, in my 20's, my priorities and mindset were totally different. I wouldn't say I was disciplined, just determined to create the best life for my son. Being a single mother, in college, working full time on night shift for a while, was such a challenge. I was determined that I would fulfill my dream of completing college.

At that time, I did make a difficult decision of leaving the school of my choice to come back home to be closer to my family for that support system. I took a year off from school after my son was born and enrolled in a University closer to home. I really wanted to go back to NC State. Although I tried to place the blame on someone else for me not returning, I had to accept full responsibility in my decision. I could have chosen to go back with my son and put a plan and schedule in place to be successful. But, leaving my son to be raised by my mother or family was not an option.

I still remember traveling back and forth to see my old college friends on many occasions, and every drive back home I cried. I cried because I was disappointed in myself for not taking the risk and going back to school at State versus settling to attend a college that I simply went to classes and had no social bond or connection. It saddens me even more that I don't even remember any of my classmates that I attended college with at UNC Charlotte. I spent most of my days on campus going to class. I was sleep deprived from working night shifts and having to take care of my son somewhere in between. For the first 3-4 years of my son's life, he had to share me with school and my job. I depended heavily on my mom and sisters to help raise my son.

They were my true backbone.

After graduating from college, my first job was in retail management. If you know anything about retail, you know that it is equivalent to long hours and varying schedules. So here I am a college graduate, and a mother still unable to provide some stability in my son's life. After a year of working retail, I decided that I needed to find a job in my field of study. After several rejected applications with the County, I was finally able to get an interview which started a new career path and chapter for me and my son. A position with the county, working a set day shift schedule, closer to home, and my son's school. But, life continued to happen.

After years of struggling in a relationship that was not healthy for my son and I; I decided to move away from my comfort zone that could have potentially been my dead zone. I was broken spiritually and mentally. So rather than allow myself to fold, give up, and continue to fight someone else's battles; I made a decision to walk away. More like runaway. I believe, at that time I decided to put it in God's hands.

I applied for another county job, closer to my older sister, and got the position after my initial interview. Working for a more diverse group of individuals was uplifting. The previous county I worked for was not diverse, especially in their management positions. I felt I would be recognized for my hard work from a more diverse team versus a team filled with people who were not culturally relevant.

I remember working hard on a state project, meeting the deadline for mandatory processing, and watching my Caucasian supervisor take all the credit. I was now working for a county that

I knew appreciated my hard work, and recognized my talents, which allowed me to be promoted quickly into a management position.

Making the decision to remove myself from a toxic relationship and from a stagnant job, allowed me to position myself for greater possibilities. The decision provided me the comfort of knowing that my Creator had a plan for my life; and in the midst of the storm there was calmness.

I was able to purchase my first home as a single mother. I even went back to school and this time I was able to mentally and physically be present in the moment. Being an older adult in college, I appreciated the value of the education process; and even more so the value of the dollar. I had to pay for my Nursing education because I had maxed out my student loans with my undergraduate degree. Nursing and caring for others are my passions.

Fast forward to today; as a wife and a new mother in my 40's, I am grateful for the journey. Even when I wanted to give up and throw in every towel I owned, I kept pressing through. My mindset was just a simple reminder to move forward and push to press upward. As I plant seeds to build my legacy, my dream is to be a full-time entrepreneur. This would allow me to pave a way for other young adults to know they can work around and through obstacles.

As I reclaim my life, and walk into my journey of entrepreneurship, I selflessly want to be a servant to assist others. Even as I Realtor, I plan to ensure I contribute with helping others fulfill their dreams of homeownership. Being unable to pay my rent at times, I know the struggles of what one may be going through and find empathy in that situation. I believe the mind is a powerful tool that can either destroy our will to live, or capture each day of the beautiful life ahead. I choose to discipline my mind, body, and soul to be great. *For the spirit God gave us does not make us timid, but gives us power, love, and self-discipline.* (Timothy 1:7) What do you choose?

INTERNAL REFLECTION QUESTIONS:

How are you shifting your mindset in regards to fine-tuning consistent discipline in your life?

_____

_____

_____

_____

_____

How does discipline relate to your "why"?

_____

_____

_____

_____

_____

Do you believe your discipline has an effect on building your legacy?

_____

_____

_____

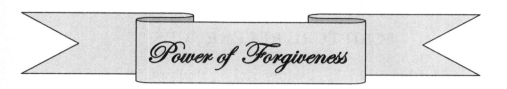

Power of Forgiveness

By: Patsy Clowney Bloom & Verganell Thomas Craig

Forgiveness is the act of excusing or pardoning others in spite of their slights shortcomings, and errors. As a theological term, forgiveness teaches us that God completely forgives sin. The initiative comes from Him because He is ready to forgive and He is a God of grace and pardon.

Sin deserves divine punishment because it is a violation of God's Holy character. However, His pardon is gracious and the sinner must come to God's sacrifice in a spirit of repentance and faith. God's forgiveness of us demands that we forgive others because grace brings responsibility and obligation.

Jesus placed no limits on the extent to which Christians are to forgive others. A forgiving spirit shows that one is a true follower of Christ. Though we may never receive an apology for what we perceived as wrong doing, forgiveness heals the wound.

God forgives us daily and we should not hold grudges, they only make things worse. Doing so gives the devil free reign to play with our thoughts. Holding on to unforgiveness is giving the other person control over us. We remain miserable while those whom we are harboring unforgiveness for are going on with life having fun. Forgive them, forgive yourself, and move on.

SCRIPTURE REFERENCES

Matthew 6:14-15, Psalms 51:1-9, Philippians 2:3

STARING INTO THE FACE OF FORGIVENESS

By: Crystal M. Edwards

Stage 1: Hurt

Hatred stirs up strife, but love covers all offenses. Proverbs 10:12

I did one last turn around at 4848, reliving every day that we spent there as husband and wife. Looking where the sofa used to be, the dining room where we had moved the table around a thousand times, the corner where we put the new entertainment set and 32-inch television with cable. That was a treat after we stuck to a budget and saved up for it. Now, as I looked around there was nothing left. This nothing was not only characterized by the empty rooms within the house, it mirrored the same nothing-ness of our marriage. Gone.

April 15, 1995 was the day we'd move into 4848 with our 2-year-old son and newborn baby girl. This had always been my fairytale: the marriage, the husband, and the children. In that order. It was the Biblical way I had been taught. The excitement of having a new home was a blessing! Loving my family, creating meals, keeping our home spotless, and being a good wife and mother was my daily routine. Then one day, it all changed. One day, we did not want the same things.

I looked at the steps and remembered. I looked at the phone jack and remembered the calls from other women. I walked through the kitchen and remembered the dinners that he did not show up for as the children and I waited. Walking through the bedrooms I remembered the joys of intimacy and the pains of sleepless nights. In the still of the quiet, I was smelling what was now our past. The end of our fairytale. As I closed the front door, for the last time, I could not look back. I smiled at my 6-year-old son and 4-year-old daughter. I still had our two babies that we had when we unloaded the boxes into the house from the first moving truck. He now had four.

The mailbox lid was down to remind me of the envelope that was in my purse. I did not want to get all the way down to our new house, back in the DMV, and realize I had never placed it in the mailbox. Sidelines, a poem I had written the week before while listening to Maxwell's Urban Suite, was in the envelope. It read….

Sidelines:

Always loved him, the coach
Since the day I was drafted on our college campus,
There was always trouble lurking with new players,
But I pressed forward
With him, the coach.
Coach still used his old playbook though.
Same game, with new players.
Coach and I have a connection
Getting' us through Hell and back

For seven seasons I was the Heissman winner
getting fully dressed
Awaiting my turn to get in the game!

Not just during intermission,
Commercial breaks
Off season
Or a short pause for 'da cause…
I want to be in the game for the duration
LIFE
A Helpmate
To help coach bring his dreams to fruition
Forming an everlasting team
Of two
That can't be stopped!
Folks always lookin'
At his left hand,
To see if we already won championship rings!

My heart is with coach
I love him
On his most evil of days
I remain loyal
I try not to anger him….
Coach, can I be free to speak my mind
Be human
With flaws
Without thinkin' my contract is up
It's stressful
'cus my contract was voided on several occasions
When coach got angry
When I signed up
I was very clear,
Understood the small print,
Legal terms
And bonding agreements
I understood that change is inevitable
And coach is human
I'm the quarterback for his team!

Now on his sideline!
There for him and the other players!
Down to make the calls in his absence!
Wanting on him to put me back in the game
I want in!

So,
I am on the sideline
Waiting for release out of my contract
voided
My stats are through the roof
Yet,
Coach has new players
To help him win another championship…
In his heart of hearts,
He knows the player that I am.
I have exposed myself to him, plenty
He remains the coach

I agree,
Lately my motivation
declining
coach yells,
that I'm not playing to my potential
Got hurt in the game
I can't ignore my physical need
Can't live without that physical touch
From coach
Any longer
Frustration with my doctors
To find a cure
Of the never-ending cycle…
That goes on, on, on
Something is not right!
I see red

Monthly
daily
why I am so tried
why so much pain
I'm depleted!
I still get in the game
daily
I am scared of my prognosis
Too scared to tell coach
Might be replaced in the new season
The sidelines are killing me.
Working so hard
trying to get
Coach's attention…
With a contract deadline looming
I continue to play at my own risk
But he can't hear me…
He still questions last season's loss
Even if it's a new day…

But I stayed on the sideline
Hoping he'd remember our Super Bowls
Wishing he'd remember the draft of 1992
Praying he'd get his plays right
For another chance to win
So that we can both go back to enjoying our **'rings'**

Stage 2: Hate

Whoever says he is in the light and hates his brother is still in darkness. 1
John 2:9

In the days after I left 4848, I reminisced on how I had found out about his other life. I would be in constant prayer and fasting that he would be hit by a train. That someone would walk up to him and blow his brains out, right in front of me, so I could see his hurt up close. It brought me joy to think that he would die. Internally, I could feel the anger churning slowly. Maybe, I would kill him myself. I had missed the perfect opportunity during the baby shower and other occasions. I could have chalked it up to the legal term, '*Hot Blood Law*,' where my emotions were so enraged, due to an immediate and present incident, that I could kill him and only get probation. One thing I knew for sure was if God granted me another chance to complete the mission of his certain and immediate death, I WOULD NOT FAIL.

My mind wondered like clockwork when there was the usual knock at the door at 6 pm on Wednesdays. It was him, the cheater, the other children's father, the "forsaker"...the dead man walking. Our babies were ready to go with their father for his agreed upon time. I was lifeless. Staring at the wall. His attempt to speak to me fell on deaf ears.

Tears began to stream down my face as I thought about the vows we made to one another; how I was supporting him in all areas; and how he treated me like I was the bottom of his shoe. And for what? Nothing! He knew that I was a good wife at only 24 years old. Without warning, the next thing I knew, my body was shaking as if something was inside of me that I could not control. I was acting on my fantasies. My body had leaped off the couch, issuing him a critical beat down in an attempt to kill him. Within minutes, it was an all-out brawl fueled by hurt, devastation, uncontrolled anger, utter embarrassment and, of course, the enemy. God intervened.

Someone was yelling my name, right against my ear. They were embracing me as I fell to the floor in a fetal position. He was standing over me crying, apologizing, and in shock. He had

NEVER seen me like that. Neither had she. It was my neighbor from two doors down, who I knew nothing about except she was a wife, a mother of one baby boy and two little girls; who drove an old, baby blue Cutlass that was three years my junior.

Why was she here? What had she seen? I was in a dark void, but I could hear her saying to him, *"This is what you have done to her. You have forsaken your good wife. The past month, I haven't seen you, but I have seen your wife, decline, but NEVER skip a beat with raising your children."* I heard him let a sob. I knew he finally understood. She asked him to leave and get our babies who she had eased into her house during the brawl. He complied.

She laid on the floor next to me as I was asking God to grant his death, again. She said in a firm voice, "GET UP. Get up, now." I was annoyed yet stunned that her demeanor had changed so quickly. *"You will never utter those words again. Ever. We do not fight the enemy through more evil in this game of spiritual warfare; we fight the enemy through prayer and FORGIVENESS. In order for you to heal and be made whole, you MUST forgive him. It is a matter of your own life and death."*

"He destroyed our family. He made me a laughing stock. He betrayed us. But I have to forgive him!" Every day, she came over and prayed with me. We read scripture. I cried. As a day turned into months, I prayed for him.

Stage 3: Hook

"Come to me, all you who are weary and burdened, and I will give you rest."
Matthew 11:28

Time was truly filled with swift transition. In my initial time of transitioning into forgiveness, my hurt superseded the focus on my actual forgiveness. It was more robotic than transparent. Even though I was in prayer, I was lost in a darkness, a void if you will, after the incident. My mind was a slave to reliving the nightmare of the baby shower and playing out all the adulterous things that he did that I did not know about. Dreams of millions of people pointing their fingers at me while laughing hysterically filled my days and nights. I was ashamed and angry.

One day, while praying, I began to beg God to come and wrap his arms around me, because I wanted to die. I drifted off to sleep. To this day, I don't know whether I was in a dream or awake, but I lifted my head to see a shadowy figure with all white, flowy garments on, positioned on the side of my bed. The feeling was so comforting and peaceful. I felt no heartbreak or anger. The figure told me to not be ashamed or hurt - all things work together for those who love Him – I was loved and to wipe my tears.

I knew it was God. I never replied. My mouth could not move. I simply laid my body back down. Over time, I began to have focused prayers to forgive. They allowed for deep healing and alleviation of the hurt that kept me awake at night - but it had NOT been instant. It took time. He never had to ask me for forgiveness; simply, I whole-heartedly gave it to him. No questions asked.

Stage 4: Heal

And whenever you stand praying, forgive, if you have anything against anyone, so that your Father also who is in heaven may forgive you your trespasses."
Mark 11:25

When God says that He will make those who have wronged you, your footstools, believe Him. When you open your heart to fully forgive, you understand that it is truly a matter of life and death. I chose to LIVE! My hurt was not about him as a person, they were about the spiritual warfare and influence of the enemy! We have all battled with spiritual warfare and influence of the enemy, but those who entertain it longer, pay a bigger price. The enemy cheated him out of his family and that was his lesson to learn. ***My lesson was to truly FORGIVE in order to truly LIVE; to truly HEAL!***

Reference: Rothberg, S. (2015) Four Stages of Forgiveness.

INTERNAL REFLECTION QUESTIONS:

The Bible says that forgiveness is a matter of life and death. Are choosing to live or die? Explain your answer.

_____

_____

_____

_____

_____

How would you define forgiveness?

_____

_____

_____

_____

_____

Is forgiving yourself (self-forgiveness) harder than forgiving someone who hurt you?

_____

_____

_____

_____

_____

FORGIVENESS: MY TRUTH

By: Alma R. Atkinson

My beginning began before it began. Jeremiah says, The word of the LORD came to me, saying, *"Before I formed you in the womb I knew you, before you were born I set you apart; I appointed you as a prophet to the nations." "Alas, Sovereign LORD," I said, "I do not know how to speak; I am too young." But the LORD said to me, "Do not say, 'I am too young.' You must go to everyone I send you to and say whatever I command you. Do not be afraid of them, for I am with you and will rescue you," declares the LORD."*

The Kingdom Principle that served as a thorn, guidance, and deliverance for me was, forgiveness. When I reflect on my life's journey, specifically, a point in time in my childhood, it began for me when I was ten years old. I was a little girl who felt abandoned by my mother. My ten-year-old self did not comprehend that Mommy did not leave on her own. The impact of my feelings and how they influenced my journey was not fully known until I revisited that little girl and owned her decisions as an adult.

I grew up to become an adult woman, journeying through unforgiveness. My feelings of abandonment, rejection, bitterness, rebellion, love-seeking, lack of confidence, offense, and exclusion were not always something I understood or knew how to process inside.

My God-fearing, praying, compassionate, by-the-Book missionary, grandmother raised my siblings and I with love. While she was a faithful seasoned Saint, my personal journey did not exclude me from life experiences and the feelings that I had.

My feelings of abandonment and the spirits that attached to me were real, and I sought to change that. The void of losing my mom was deep. Although she did not reject me, that is what I felt. Although I was loved, I did not always feel the agape love and did not always have the tools to give it.

Although, I knew that God was working on the inside of me to work some things out of me, some of the trials and tribulations that I experienced fed those negative feelings. Sometimes the situations were similar but wherever I went, I ALWAYS showed up. I knew that the answer was in God and that He would lead the way. I knew that the foundation was laid for me; it was up to me to continue to build my relationship with God and seek God through His promises to and for me.

Interestingly, when others experienced loss, God would use me to encourage them. When people were hurt or betrayed, God would use me to encourage them. When people were hopeless, God would use me as a vessel of hope. I became an encourager, intercessor, peace-maker, and helper to others.

I now see that God was building me up in my most holy faith; not because I had it all together, but because He has it all together. God was framing my endurance in a way that only He would get the glory. I cannot do this journey called life apart from my Lord and Savior, Jesus Christ.

I can recall finding a letter that spoke about me in a way that was hurtful at that time. I can recall being the only loved one excluded from an event. When I reflect on my feelings and being excluded, I know now it was necessary. The necessity did not exempt me from pain. In the deep pain, I became the encourager, the nurturer, and the helper. As a more mature vessel, I have learned that exclusion is sometimes God's protection.

Through life's journey, as I matured in Christ and became more surrendered, something could happen and I would ask myself, *what is that about?* This is when I became convicted. Even though I knew I had forgiven others, the conflict on the inside said otherwise, I was picking stuff back up.

The Bible says to forgive others to be forgiven and if I did not forgive, I would not be forgiven. According to John 1:5, *"the light shines in the darkness, and the darkness has not overcome it."* I was not exempt from fully forgiving others. Jesus had forgiven me. If I wanted to be forgiven, I had to forgive.

My journey was necessary to be able to now share from a place of deliverance. For me, the difference of true forgiveness was forgiving and not picking the issue back up. When my soul cried out for change, God began leveling me through deliverance. I did not want to be stuck. Based on my decisions, I wanted God's best for my life and a Kingdom legacy of generational blessings for my family. Therefore, I became more intentional about doing things differently.

To be more intentional, I became more attuned to what God was doing. This involved a series of leveling for me. As I reflect, I see that God was strategic when I showed up. God's leveling process for me included divine connections and God-ordained encounters. The leveling process that God took me through included me showing up for my deliverance.

Along with prayer and devotion, there were specific gatherings; face-to-face and online that the Holy Spirit led me to partake in. Each time I moved, I knew God was working on the inside of me. I had to make a decision to receive God's whole Word on the Kingdom Principle of forgiveness.

I had to make a decision to forgive and release. When I went through deliverance, I forgave. I released. I received my deliverance. The truest test of my deliverance has been, being faced with a situation pre-deliverance; and my reaction being faced with the same or a similar situation post-deliverance and my reaction.

God is so amazing. Truly, *"for it is God who works in you to will and to act in order to fulfill his good purpose."* Philippians 2:13. The test of my deliverance is not what I can do in my own strength; it is what I can do in the strength that God has given me through Jesus Christ.

I had to know what God's Word said about forgiveness. I had to pray. I had to be available and open to the process in God's shifting. I had to be obedient. I had to be transformed and renewed in my mind. I had to surrender. All of this is still true today.

As I sought the Lord, I continued to grow in Him as a disciple in the Body of Christ within and beyond the four walls of the church. God began to manifest opportunities for me including: new divine relationships, women gatherings at my church, the call to ministry, the 21 Day Awakening Journey, The Awakening Encounter, Heart 2 Heart 31 Day Transformational Daily Devotional, The Unlocking Destiny Conference, and the Keep It Moving (K.I.M.) Mentoring Program. These were all encounters that God called me by name to experience and I showed up available to His call. I had to acknowledge the sin, cry out to God for forgiveness, forgive others, help free others, and be free myself.

The deliverance process began to occur when I acknowledged or questioned my feelings. Proverbs 4:23 NIV says, *"Above all else, guard your heart, for everything you do flows from it."* I accepted that there were some unguarded things in me and in my heart that I needed for God to root out of me. By faith, I began to seek after the change.

When God would place an open door before me, I would walk through. This included a series of God-ordained encounters that God would show me, including one when I made a decision to go to a weekend away; Ordained by God, facilitated by my mentor Pastor Kimberly Jones, and led by the Holy Spirit with other sisters. My heart and spirit were ripe for what God did that weekend. I had gone through the layering and I was now in a place of leveling. I absolutely had no idea what to expect during that weekend. I fully expected God to move.

Through my deliverance, I went back again and was honest with God and with myself of what I felt. Mind you, I thought I had dealt with my issues. That probably was my issue, I had dealt with them myself and not allowed God to deal with me. In an atmosphere that was set for deliverance, my heart was pliable to cry out to God. Through my deliverance process, I had to deal with unforgiveness.

Through my deliverance process of forgiveness, I have grown in my faith, matured in my endurance, and gained a deeper understanding that the ways and thoughts of God are so much higher than mine. I lived through it, to God be all the glory!!! Romans 1:17 says, *"For therein is the righteousness of God revealed from faith to faith: as it is written, The just shall live by faith."*

Those chains of unforgiveness in my past no longer have me bound. When faced with an adverse situation, I see it as a present situation. I acknowledge it, forgive, and seek God for His help; and each time I give God the glory for delivering me.

Be encouraged in knowing there is nothing unknown to God about any of us. Seek God for His knowledge, wisdom, and understanding. Lean not to your own understanding. God desires a relationship with us. We can cast our cares upon Him.

However you've journeyed to your current plight, God already knows. His ear is inclined to you. Cry out to God about your unforgiveness. Ask Him to deliver you from sin, forgive others, release them, and free yourself from the burden that Jesus already paid for us at Calvary. I John 1:9 says, *"If we confess our sins, he is faithful and just to forgive us our sins, and to cleanse us from all unrighteousness."*

As children of the Most High, expect opposition but know the Victory is already won. When trials and tribulations come, and they will, retreat in God. Trust YOUR God-ordained process. *"Trust in the Lord with all your heart and lean not on your own understanding; in all your ways submit to him, and he will make your paths straight."* Proverbs 3:5-6

INTERNAL REFLECTION QUESTIONS:

What unforgiveness in your past are you carrying?

_____

_____

_____

_____

_____

Will you forgive to become free of the sin of unforgiveness?

_____

_____

_____

_____

_____

How often should we forgive and be forgiven?

_____

_____

_____

_____

_____

FORGIVENESS IS THE ART OF LIFE

By: ULanda R. Hunter

Note to my 5-year-old self!

I just want to let you know that life will happen to you. You are going to experience things you have no control over. You are going to have adults that will fail you in life.

Don't be afraid; there will be people who will violate your innocence. You will have a baby very young; it's okay she will turn out just fine. You will make some very bad decisions in life. You are going to be a high school dropout.

You will get married and have other children. You will get a divorce. You and your children will struggle for a while and you will feel helpless as a mother. You will even be judged on your parenting. But I want to let you know that it will pass, and your children will be success stories.

Oh, I forgot to tell you, you will experience a lot of different abuse and violence in your life. This will only make you stronger and more resilient. As if that's not enough, you will become severely depressed and even contemplate taking your own life. But God will intervene and send someone to pray for you and with you. Even though you will question your existence and be confused about your life's purpose; things will surprisingly turn around and be okay.

I want you to know that you will survive and come out victorious. Guess what? You will get a GED and later successfully earn a master's degree. Life will be about overcoming obstacles and having moments of sadness. But, that happiness will lead to some joyful life-altering moments.

Forgiveness, Was for Me.

Often you go through life just thinking, why me? Why did I get chosen for this life? Why could I not be the one to who was chosen to be entitled? Entitled meaning born with certain rights or privileges inherited or by stature. Why couldn't I have been gifted with obvious talents like a singer, a model, a movie star, or just be rich or something? That's what most people think or at least what I thought. I used to believe that if I was any of those things, it wouldn't come with baggage or problems. I was always questioning God about my circumstances in life.

I was saved at 9 years old. I went to church every Sunday, attended Sunday School, Bible study and choir rehearsals. My church was literally around the corner from where I lived. God knew His plans for my life. I had no clue what life would be like for me. What I can tell you is, I experienced a lot of hurt.

My life was predestined by God. God knew His plans for me. He knew I would have a lot of wilderness moments that I would need to travel through to get to where I am today. 2 King 3:8 states, *And he said, Which way shall we go up? And he answered, The way through the wilderness of Edom.* (KJV). Basically, life was not going to be all good, I had to go through in order to 'grow through.' My 'grow through' was the art of forgiveness.

My experiences of being hurt by people I thought had my best interest in life was shocking for me. I needed to learn to forgive them in order to move forward. I questioned God again, "how does forgiveness help me and why should I forgive someone who hurt me?"

Some of my wilderness experiences of hurt prepared me to be brave and bold enough to forgive. I realized that if I can get through the hurt, process the hurt; then, I can forgive the hurt. I began to understand that my hurt was only a moment in time. I had to recognize moments of time in my life as just moments and not my whole entire life. If I allowed those hurt moments to take root in my life it would have affected my ability to function mentally, physically, and spiritually. My life would have been held hostage by not being able to forgive. I had the control to define the outcome of my hurt and I chose to move forward, not backward, and not to stand still.

I cannot explain my childhood in full ,but knowing how I grew up and my childhood experiences set the tone for some of the choices I made later in life. I grew up thinking that my life was normal, but it was very dysfunctional which became normalized. I was used to the dysfunctions and my life was not much different than that of other families that lived in my neighborhood.

I grew up in the projects in South Central LA and I got into a lot of fights. I've seen a lot of horrible things happen to good people in my community. There was very little policing for what needed policing and over policing on everything else. What I saw or experienced is now labeled "trauma". When I began to stack up all my experiences, domestic violence, molestation, childhood exposures, broken friendships, a failed marriage, and broken romantic relationships, I knew I was very damaged. Later, that hurt turned to bitterness and unforgiveness.

I watched TV a lot and I watched shows exemplifying the white family lifestyle, like, *The Brady Bunch, I Dream of Jeanie,* and *Leave It to Beaver.* I also watched shows portraying the Black family lifestyle of struggling and living in the hood, such as, *Good Times* and *What's Happening.* While raising my family I would watch the *Cosby Show* and a *Different World.* As I grew up, I would dream of what my life would be like in the future. I wanted a family like the ones on TV. I hung on to this dream for a long time, until I realized that most dreams do not come true.

I was a teen mom at 16 years old. At that time the only practice I had of being a mother was playing with dolls. I had no real clue on what it took to be a mother, but I had to figure it out.

What I did know was I had to protect her and keep her safe. I did not want what happened to me to happen to her. So everywhere I went she was on my hip because I didn't trust anyone to babysit her.

Teenage pregnancy forced me to be on my own from an early age. I didn't have any good role models to help me understand healthy relationships, friendships, and life. I had to just figure it out. Friends, back then, weren't much help because they had their own problems. I also had to learn that "friends" will share your business with others – especially if there is a falling out and the friendship breaks down.

I eventually got married and had two more children. My marriage was nothing like the ones I had seen on TV - and I mean nothing like it. We made the best of it. But neither of us knew what a healthy relationship was, and by extension a healthy marriage. This is when I began to learn that the people closest to you will hurt you the most. You may ask what you mean, let me explain.

I thought being married would alleviate a lot of my problems. I thought I would worry less about things. That I had a protector, provider, and someone who loved me no matter what and life would just be easier; that was somewhat true. However, it came with other things too, things that I was not prepared to handle.

I could write a book on what not to do in a marriage, but this is not the book. Let me say this, I learned I had a whole lot of trust, faith, and dependency on my husband and not a lot on God. My ex-husband was just as unequipped as me. When things started to fall apart, I was hurt deeply and almost turned my back on God. I blamed God because I thought I was the perfect Christian woman, wife, and mother and He allowed me to be hurt by my husband. Who was I to blame God? Especially since warning comes before destruction, and we were both warned.

Due to a build-up of unhealthy circumstance and a lack of trust, I left my husband. I was so damaged and did not know what I wanted in a relationship. Despite that, I found myself in several relationships thereafter that were equally unhealthy. My heart had truly been broken several times and this led to a feeling of unworthiness, feeling inferior, vulnerable, scared, and like I had to overcompensate in other areas of my life.

The hurt caused a void in my life. The hurt took root and started affecting me in all areas. I was often quick to anger and had limited ability to process what I was truly feeling. I found myself feeling depressed often and not understanding why. I was very guarded, and somewhat I'm still guarded, especially when thinking about getting involved in a relationship with a man.

I was allowing my past hurt to create feelings of sadness and complete hopelessness. I was feeling like something was wrong with me and that no man could truly love me. I was feeling like I was nothing and that even my children didn't like me.

When you are hurting because you feel someone has caused it, you become helpless, at least I was, and I wanted them to hurt too. I learned what I always knew deep down; God had chosen me just like He had chosen Jesus. Even Jesus, cried out to God, At the ninth hour, *Jesus cried out in a loud voice, "Eloi, Eloi, lema sabachthani?"* which means, *"My God, My God, why have You forsaken Me?"(Mark 15:34)*.

My hurt was so much at times, I felt crucified and contemplated why am I here. But God knew what my life experiences would be and being saved at nine, in some way, made me strong; and guided me through it all and kept me. If I can quote T.D. Jakes, *"You don't have enough strengths to manage yesterday's hurt."* Me being saved built up strength in me to handle all of the wilderness moments that were going to cause me to hurt.

God knew I could handle the hurt and that my hurt experiences would help someone else through their hurt experiences; and they would need the strengths and encouragement to get through. With my help, they would be able to pass along encouragement to someone else who needs the support in " a pay it forward" kind of way, but with God.

The beginning of my forgiveness journey

I was invited to join a Christian women's support group, which became instrumental in my healing. My journey to forgiveness started when I went to a Christian women's retreat. It came to that part of the service where if you wanted prayer you could wait in line for individual prayer. I didn't need to go up there because I prayed for myself and I have my own personal relationship with God. My thoughts were, *"let others who really need prayer go up there."*

After the prayers were over, the minister for that night said, "someone is battling depression and it's on and off." I was still in the spirit praising and worshipping God when the minister walked towards me.

Let me be honest, I considered myself to be a strong Christian, back then and now. I was hesitant because I don't like open prophecy. I was obedient and I allowed her to minister to me. She quietly talked with me and I listened. She prayed and I prayed with her for my deliverance.

A part of what God gave her to share with me was that " [I] need[ed] to let go of the past, the hurt and that it [was] okay to let it go, because it was causing [me] to be depressed and God did not save [me] to be in that state of mind".

How did forgiveness become essential in my life?

After the retreat, the women's group did a study on forgiveness, how ironic. We studied from the book *"Total Forgiveness" by R. T. Kindle.* This book along with the supportive women in the group was instrumental in my healing regarding forgiveness. I really learned a lot. Mainly how I needed to forgive myself and that forgiveness isn't for the other person, but for me. I prayed and read, prayed some more and read, and then I started to practice forgiveness.

Little by little I understood why I should forgive me. I learned that, by holding on to the hurt; I was holding on to unforgiveness in my heart. But my heart was not clear of the issues that were plaguing us. That unforgiveness was preventing me from letting go of the hurt, the book *"Total Forgiveness"* references this in a chapter titled *"Signs that I haven't forgiven myself."* Imagine me thinking I had it all together, a strong Christian woman, and had no clue that the jest or root cause of most of my problems stemmed from unforgiveness.

I discovered that I was a "wounded Christian". *Matthew 6: 14 – 15 "For if you forgive other people when they sin against you, your heavenly Father will also forgive you. ¹⁵ But if you do not forgive others their sins, your Father will not forgive your sins."* I was so hurt, and it truly affected all areas of my life, work, children, social, friendships, and relationships. I was angry a lot. Psalms 37:8 states, *"Refrain from anger and turn from wrath; do not fret—it leads only to evil".* I am almost sure I was hurting other people that were in my life too; such as my children, family, friends, and co-workers.

The book took me through exercises that forced me to reflect on my life and the hurtful things that took root in my heart and mind. Unforgiveness was consuming me and I did not even know or recognize it. I had to recognize that if I wanted to get better, I needed to find a way to forgive and I was secretly wanting those who hurt me to feel hurt too.

I was interfering with God's job by "playing God" and guess what else? Yep! I was blocking my own fellowship and anointing. At the end of the day, I was only hurting myself. 1 John 1:6 reminded me, *"If we claim to have fellowship with him and yet walk in the darkness, we lie and do not live out the truth" NIV.* The book refers to this as "The Art of Forgiving and Forgetting." My healing included forgiving those who I felt had done me wrong. Without being able to do that, I could not receive my healing in forgiveness.

My mind was playing tricks on me and my heart was throbbing with pain from the build-up of heartache, childhood memories, adulthood…life! Once, I began to pray and understand the importance of forgiveness, I began to feel a release in my life. It literally felt like chains were falling off.

I started to feel better emotionally, physically, and in my thoughts. I prayed more and prayed sincerely for those that I blamed for hurting me. I also prayed for the ability to forgive myself. Of course, I blamed myself too. I needed to forgive myself for being human. There is nothing like being hurt by someone you love or care for deeply or thinking you, meaning me, contributed to the hurt.

Staying on Track

I still have flashbacks when certain things trigger me. When I find myself in situations where people don't appreciate me or treat me like what I have done doesn't matter, that can be hurtful and will trigger me.

"Therefore, as God's chosen people, holy and dearly loved, clothe yourselves with compassion, kindness, humility, gentleness, and patience. Bear with each other and forgive one another if any of you has a grievance against someone. Forgive as the Lord forgave you. And over all these virtues put on love, which binds them all together in perfect unity. Let the peace of Christ rule in your hearts, since as members of one body you were called to peace. And be thankful." Colossians 3:12-15

I had to learn to believe and stand on the Word of God for my life. I had to understand that things I'd been through and will go through are a trial and test of my faith and love for God. I needed to trust God to do what He said He would do; by allowing Him to be my source and strength.

I had to come to the realization that I can stand boldly before others and share how God has delivered me. Forgiveness also taught me not to have expectations of people; because my expectations may not be something they can give. I realized that I have my own expectations of myself and that is what I govern myself by.

God gives me things that apply to me. He gives other people what applies to them. For me to stay on track, I learned not to focus on what I expect from others, then I won't be hurt if they cannot deliver. I almost got myself caught up in that unforgiveness cycle again. I was having all kinds of mental conversations with myself, but God took me back to "unforgiveness". I stay praying because I didn't want unforgiveness to creep back into my heart, forcing me to process through my feelings and why.

I also know that if I do not take time to fellowship with God, I will be back in that bitter, dark, sad, worthless state of mind again; feeling guilty and having a pity party for myself. I want nothing more but to have peace with God through all my trials and tribulations, once again, reminding myself that everything is only a test. I do not want to harbor unforgiveness; that is definitely a sin against God.

Therefore, since we have been justified through faith, we have peace with God through our Lord Jesus Christ, through whom we have gained access by faith into this grace in which we now stand. And we boast in the hope of the glory of God. Not only so, but we also glory in our sufferings, because we know that suffering produces perseverance; perseverance, character; and character, hope. And hope does not put us to shame, because God's love has been poured out into our hearts through the Holy Spirit, who has been given to us. Romans 5:1-5

The art of practicing forgiveness, for me, includes alleviating expectations that I may have of others towards me. It requires me to focus on my own expectations and focus on my own moral responsibilities. It challenges me to take charge of how I react in any situation. When I can do this, I have a quicker bounce back; knowing that I am responsible for how I choose to move forward after someone, or some situation causes me pain.

When practicing forgiveness, things want to rest in me and take root then, they begin to sprout into unforgiveness. It was hard for me to forgive people who had deliberately hurt me and those who unknowingly hurt me. It was a process and it was hard to let go.

I thought of ways that I could get back at others, but I know that it was not of God. After learning that forgiveness was for me and only me, I had to tarry through the process. When I tarried through, I readily took the journey for my healing from unforgiveness. I did what I needed to do to get deliverance from unforgiveness which included: praying regularly, reading my bible and other self-help books, processing the word of God, journaling, crying and worshipping. Knowing that my strength comes from God, *I can do all this through him who gives me strength."* *(Philippians 4:13)* God can make the impossible possible if I trust Him. Matthew 19:26 informs us, *"But Jesus looked at them and said to them, "With men this is impossible, but with God all things are possible."*

I know now that I desire forgiveness and when life happens, as it will; I can forgive, forget and move on. I have a God-given strength in me.

INTERNAL REFLECTION QUESTIONS:

What does the word forgiveness mean in your life? How can you apply that forgiveness in your life?

_____

_____

_____

_____

_____

As you look back over your life, think about areas where you have been hurt and what steps can you take to apply forgiveness?

_____

_____

_____

_____

_____

We often blame ourselves when others hurt us. Please make a forgiveness list of things you forgive yourself for.

_____

_____

_____

_____

_____

Power of Apology

By: Patsy Clowney Bloom & Verganell Thomas Craig

Apology is written or spoken expression of one's regret, remorse, or sorrow for having insulted, failed, injured or wronged another.

A genuine, real, apology is more than just a confession or wrongdoing; it is a request for mercy and forgiveness. Apology is a humbling act. It can very challenging. However, when we know that we have wronged someone, be it knowingly or unknowingly, it is imperative that we apologize from our hearts.

Simply apologizing because someone told you to without understanding the error of your ways is not transformative. To grow, we have to accept the fact that we were wrong, or just misunderstood. Apology is necessary and an effective mechanism for divine flow as we journey.

Saying I am sorry is just as important for you as it is for the other person. Usually, when you harm someone with actions or words you know by the conviction. When this occurs, correct it right away. Knowing you have hurt someone is a hindrance to your spiritual journey. You can't move forward with a clear conscience.

Apology is not always to another person, yet is most effective when we can apologize to ourselves and forgive ourselves for our former selves.

SCRIPTURE REFERENCES

Romans 12:18, Proverbs 15:18, Exodus 34:6

APOLOGY-JUST WHAT IS IT?

By: Yvonne Wilson Anderson

*S*ometimes having to apologize is one of the hardest things to do. However, an apology should be given as soon as an offense has occurred. Let's define just what an apology is. An apology is a statement essentially containing two keywords. It is a regretful acknowledgment for having caused an offense or failure. In a nutshell, it shows sorrow over your actions and acknowledges the hurt that these actions caused someone else.

The world would indeed be a wonderful place, if we said, *"I'm sorry, please forgive me"*, every time we offended someone. Everyone needs to know how to say *"I am sorry,"* because we are all flawed people. We all make mistakes as no one is perfect, except the Lord.

"Why do you call me good?" Jesus answered saying, "No one is good—except God alone." - Mark 11:18

Hurting other people is an equal opportunity employer and, often times, does not discriminate with age, race, or gender. Whether or not our actions or behavior intentionally hurt others, knowing how to apologize correctly to anyone we've hurt helps to restore trust and reestablish our relationship with that person.

"A person's wisdom yields patience, it is to one's glory to overlook an offense" Proverbs 19:11.

Apologizing says that we are keenly aware that our behavior was unacceptable. An apology won't resolve the conflict or take away the psychological trauma of the injury. However, it can mitigate the pain and frequently has the ability to stop the emotional bleeding. We take responsibility by speaking what is the truth. *"I acted so foolishly." "I was really nasty to you." "I was wrong and I am sorry that I offended you."* Sincerely humbling yourself by saying contrite words such as these will build trust back; provided that your actions following the apology match your regretful words. Saying you are sorry is a good place to begin the journey of reconciliation.

At this point, it helps to open a discussion on what is acceptable and what is not. Heart-centered apologies help to restore communication by promoting emotional intimacy. Admitting that what has happened between you was your fault restores dignity to the person that you have hurt. This is the most important phase in an apology.

Additionally, when you admit that the situation was your fault, it gives you the chance to play a pivotal role in the healing process. Saying *"I'm sorry"* and asking for forgiveness also makes sure that the other person doesn't unjustly blame themselves for what has happened.

Lastly, a heartfelt apology indicates that we are taking responsibility for our actions. Doing so shores up our own confidence, reputation, and respect. Most likely, we will feel better being honest and forthright about our actions.

Admitting that you were wrong takes great strength and depth of character. It involves swallowing your pride and readiness to be honest and vulnerable. Apologizing is also one of the best ways to restore your integrity with others if they witnessed the offense as well. Just remember that apologizing is the act of expressing regret or remorse for an offense that you caused.

Saying I am sorry knocks the wall of resentment down. It also allows you to begin talking to the person that you have wounded. Being able to admit your mistake gives the offended party the chance to communicate with you and thereby cope with their feelings about the issue. When you receive an apology, it validates your hurt feelings. You then feel seen, heard, and respected. You are also more readily willing to listen to the feelings and requests of the offender in return.

In the same light, not apologizing has its consequences too. You may destroy your relationships with family, friends, clients, and colleagues. I have seen what happens in the workplace when you do not apologize; it deeply harms reputations, limits career opportunities, and lowers productiveness. Other people may not want to work with a person who will not apologize, which severely limits effectiveness.

In a work situation, the negativity created deeply affects the team when you don't apologize. No one wants to work for a boss or with a co-worker who won't own up to their mistakes, and who doesn't apologize for them. The animosity, tension, and pain that comes with not apologizing will certainly create a toxic work environment.

Oftentimes, apologies are very difficult and courage must be summoned to apologize. Admitting that you were wrong, automatically places you in a vulnerable position ≈

"While Ezra was praying and confessing, weeping and throwing himself down before the house of God, a large crowd of Israelites -men, women and children gathered around him.   Psalm 25:17

They too wept bitterly."   By being vulnerable you may be exposed to attack or blame in retaliation.

Some people struggle to act courageously.   If you do not apologize, shame and embarrassment will overtake you because you are under conviction.   *"Relieve the troubles of my heart and free me from my anguish,"* (Psalm 25:17) is a verse to keep in mind; if you don't apologize you might be seen as arrogant as well.   Your reputation suffers and you will not be seen as a wise or inspiring person.

On a personal note, I was in the midst of a trial that involved an apology that had not been fully received.   I was dating a Christian gentleman, and everything was wonderful until Christmas Eve of that year. I innocently sent my friend a picture of myself, and the response that I got from him was little to nothing remotely comparable to the responses that I generally received.

I was met with harsh criticism and with the threat of breaking up.   I could not believe that I was talking to the same man who had already won my heart.   I thought someone had taken control of his voice and used it to say harsh things to me.   I tried to de-escalate the ire that was being directed towards me, but it got progressively worse.   After insulting me for several minutes, I became angry and retaliated with harsh words in return.

I said very hurtful things to him because I was so engulfed with anger due to being attacked for no reason.   As I felt anger rising within me, I heard the voice of the Lord gently telling me not to go there with him, *"In your anger do not sin. Do not let the sun go down while you are still angry."* (Ephesians 4:26) I ignored the voice and fired nuclear missiles back which devastated him even though he started the fight. Needless to say, we did not spend Christmas or the New Year together as we were not speaking to each another.

I was devastated, hurt, and inconsolable with grief over what had happened between us. I said some things to him that I had to repent for before the Lord. I got fully in the flesh and had smoke streaming out of my ears.

"My dear brothers and sisters, take note of this: Everyone should be quick to listen, slow to speak and slow to become angry." (James 1:19)

It took another seven days before any form of communication opened between us, *"so they too have now been disobedient in order that by the mercy shown to you they also may now receive mercy."* (Romans 11:31). He apologized to me and I apologized to him as well. In taking this heart matter before the Lord, our relationship was put on pause.

Both of us repented and the Lord stood between us. He began fellowshipping more with the Lord by going to church and early morning prayer more often. I stood before the Lord ministering to Him through praise and worship which sat things right within me as well. There is no darkness in God and His light flows through us casting out any darkness within us. There is no division in God's heart. He is the God of Heaven. I prayed, "Let there be light in our darkness, open our hearts to Your light. Let the light that shines from You shine in us. Jesus have your way."

A sincere apology may quicken the start of the process to finish any unfinished, emotional business in a relationship. It requires honesty, accountability, and a desire, not only for closure, but for communion. I sincerely apologized and said that I should not have said the horrible things I'd said to him. I also said that I leveled up higher than he had with insults to match those that he had said to me. Afterwards, I deeply regretted my actions towards him. You may be thinking, "but look at what he did to you." I understand that, but if God stopped loving us, He would not have sent Jesus to redeem us.

For me, the shift that the Holy Spirit was dealing with me in this situation was that I did not have to fight that fight. I should have allowed Him to contend with those that contend with me.

"Contend, Lord, with those who contend with me; fight against those who fight against me." (Psalm 35:1)

I was disobedient to the voice of the Lord and did not follow His instructions.

"But Samuel replied: 'Does the Lord delight in burnt offerings and sacrifices as much as in obeying the Lord? To obey is better than sacrifice,' and to heed is better than the fat of a ram." (Samuel 15:22)

I clearly heard the instruction but did not follow the command. I repented for my part in these awful circumstances. I know that the Lord does not deal with the other person until He deals with you first. Jesus asks this question, *"How can you think of saying to your friend, 'Let me help you get rid of that speck in your eye,' when you can't see past the log in your own eye"* (Matthew 7:4)

Since that happened, I allowed the Lord to take the log from my eye by coming before Him with praise and worship, reading and confessing the Word over my life and praying for myself and for my friends. I read devotionals centered on how to love those around me with the love of God. I rely on this lesson every time I have conflict. I now look for the way of escape without losing the grace of God. I learned through this experience that the Lord will resolve tension and conflict. I desired reconciliation so that the peace of God would be between us. However, I realized that the Lord would work the good out of this situation.

"And we know that in all things God works for the good of those who love him, who have been called according to his purpose." (Romans 8:28)

I learned a very valuable but costly lesson, which is to not to fight fire with fire and more importantly to take the high road. Even though I stood up for myself, in the heat of the moment, I went too far. I deeply regretted not listening to that still small voice speaking to my heart instructing me not react.

"I will instruct you and teach you in the way you should go; I will counsel you with my loving eye on you," Psalm 32:8

This is a heart matter and I wanted my heart to be right before the Lord. Living in the Kingdom requires obedience to the Word of God. If I had listened to the Lord, I would have been blameless in this situation and would not have suffered any consequences. I believed God for reconciliation because Luke 1:37 says, *"With God all things are possible".*

INTERNAL REFLECTION QUESTIONS:

After you apologize, would you ask, "How can I make this up to you?"

_____

_____

_____

_____

_____

If you accepted an apology from the offender, would you be able to treat them in the same manner as you did before the offense happened?

_____

_____

_____

_____

_____

After an apology, would you ask, "How are you feeling? What did I do that caused that feeling? Could I have done something differently?"

_____

_____

_____

_____

_____

THE APOLOGY THAT NEVER CAME

By: Towanda Wilson

"I never knew how strong I was until I had to forgive someone who wasn't sorry and accept an apology I never received." - Unknown

For years I had carried the guilt, shame, and fear associated with being sexually molested as a child. I was six years old when the abuse began. The first incident, "he" wanted to play a game with me, while we were waiting in the car for my mother to return from paying bills. It was a very cold, snowy day, even for a Michigan winter. As we waited for my mother to return, "he" asked me if I wanted to play a game. It started with me closing my eyes and trying to determine which key was the house key, car key, etc. The key game quickly escalated into him exposing himself and having me "guess" what it was that I was touching next. "he" stated this was to be our little secret and that my mother would be very upset with me if she found out.

That was the day that the seeds of guilt, shame, and fear from molestation were first planted into my life. Each time that I was victimized, "he" would always tell me that I was his "special" girl. But, to make sure that I didn't tell anyone our secrets, he began to threaten the life of my mother. As a child living in a home where physical abuse was taking place on a regular basis, that was the threat that silenced me the most. I witnessed my mother being dragged, kicked, slapped, and punched more times than I could count; so I knew he meant exactly what he said.

Afraid to be alone with him at any given time, I would decline rides to McDonalds and opportunities to travel with him to his sister's house to play with his niece. I attempted to accompany my mother everywhere, and insisted to be dropped off first whenever he picked up my childhood friend and I from the Boys & Girls Club. Sometimes my antics worked, and sometimes they didn't. The darkest period of that time was when I began praying to die. I didn't have a clue regarding what actions I should take to die, I just felt that it was the only way to be free of him. I thought my day of freedom finally came when my mother and he broke up and he moved out for good. But was I really free?

For years, I kept my secret of being abused hidden. It wasn't until I was twenty-one years old that my secret was revealed to my mother. She didn't hear about it from me directly. She discovered my secret by reading about it in the journal I used for expressing my thoughts. She was very distraught and blamed herself for not seeing the signs sooner. For years I blamed myself for the mental breakdown that she suffered after finding out what had happened. It would still be over twenty years before I would discover that my mother carried the same secret that I had been carrying. She too experienced what it was like to have someone take advantage of her the way that I was taken advantage of.

As I got older and became an adult, being sexually molested as a child affected me in many ways when it came to relationships. I found myself drawn to people who filled my personal voids on a temporary basis. I longed to be loved, appreciated, valued and much more. Yet, at the same time I felt that I wasn't worthy enough for any of those things whenever I was mistreated. No matter the number of times that I was shown who someone was, I always sought to find the "good" in them or desired for them to see it in me. Thinking and acting this way came at a cost. It cost me my own self-worth and a broken heart. I truly believed that if you looked in the dictionary, you would have seen my picture under the word pain, waving all the red flags that I collected along the way. That's how much I was hurting. For years I carried this pain and accepted it as a part of my identity.

At twenty-one, I was a single parent to three sons. The one thing that I wanted to give to my children was the opportunity to grow up in a household with both of their parents. Unfortunately, the day came in which I had to decide if it was worth the mental anguish that I endured in the relationship with their father. When the relationship ended, instead of taking time to heal, I jumped into another "situationship;" to prove to myself and others that a woman with three children under the age of four was worthy of being loved. I would repeat this cycle many times throughout my life. The cycle would end after facing the seasonal depression head on that tormented me each winter; which was around the time my abuse began and my marriage dissolved at the age of forty-five. Instead of running to someone to take the pain away, I chose to give it ALL to God.

The abuse not only affected the way I looked at relationships, but also my desires to have a daughter. Though I dreamed of having a daughter, I was terrified of having one. My greatest fear was not being able to protect her from the dangers that I had endured in my childhood. In 2000, God illustrated that my fears were false evidence appearing real by blessing me with my one and only daughter.

As a child, I was introduced to God and prayer. It wasn't until I was baptized, as an adult, that I was able to fully acknowledge what had happened to me. After the baptism, we were ushered into a back room and one of the mothers, Mother Bass, at the church began to pray over me and told me that God said to give my pain to Him. The pain that I experienced as a child needed to be given to Him for me to be healed.

Those words blew my mind because I never shared with anyone outside of family about the abuse. The moment I surrendered and said the words out loud, was the first time that I spoke in tongues. That day I felt as if the weight of the world had been lifted off my shoulders.

One thing that I was determined to do, if nothing else, was to prevent the generational curse of molestation and abuse from being passed on to my children. It had happened to my mother and to me, but it was NOT going to have my children. I made sure to talk to them about inappropriate touching as soon as they were able to comprehend the basic concepts about their private areas. I also made sure they were comfortable telling me any and everything when it came to anyone around them, including family. I didn't want to be naïve enough to believe that anyone would be exempt. This was not a one-time conversation either. I had it with them numerous times throughout the years.

In 2002, my children and I began attending a ministry called Beautiful Gate International Church under the leadership of Apostle Charles Dixon. It was at this church that God began truly showing me how He intended to use the pain that I experienced for his glory. One year we hosted a Women's Prayer Breakfast and though I was assisting as needed, I knew God wanted me to do more. The theme was "More Than A Conqueror" and I knew this event was going to be powerful. Minister Annette contacted me one evening and stated that God told her to call me and ask me to be one of the speakers. Before I could decline, she stated that I had a story He wanted me to share and it was time. I quickly told her I would call her back and hung up. I couldn't believe that God would tell her that! I had told Him I was never going to speak publicly about the abuse when He showed me a vision of speaking to a room filled with women years prior. However, I have come to realize the meaning behind "If you want to make God laugh, tell Him YOUR plans!"

I did speak that Saturday morning just as God ordained me to do. I prayed and meditated to Juanita Bynum's *Gospel Goes Classical CD* in preparation of the Prayer Breakfast. I trusted God to provide me with the words for my speech and help someone who may be in bondage from sexual abuse. As I reflect on that day, the word that best describes what I experienced is supernatural. After I spoke, a few women in attendance from the local homeless shelter began to approach me and thank me for sharing my story. I was surprised to know that they too were molested and that I strengthened them in sharing my testimony. I also thanked God because I could have been hooked on drugs or alcohol to numb the pain throughout the years. It was that day that I realized that God truly meant to get the glory from what the enemy meant for evil in my life.

Yet in all these things we are more than conquerors through Him who loved us. - Romans 8:37 NKJV.

I realized that to truly heal and be released from the pain of my past, I had to forgive "him". However, the question was how, and why should I forgive him for the apology that I never received? It was almost three years ago that God provided me with an answer to both questions as only He could. I located "him" on social media and though he had multiple pages, I sent the same message to all his pages through Messenger. One of the most important things from my message to him that stands out to me most is the following;

"I wanted to personally take this time to tell you that I forgive you. I forgive you not for you, but for me... Yes, I remember it all, every horrible nightmare that you committed and did to me. Every one of them that I tried to suppress and move to the farther parts of my mind. I can only assume that you too were once sexually abused by someone close to you in your past and was only repeating the cycle, the generational curse. I only hope that you have repented and asked God for forgiveness. However, at this time I FORGIVE YOU! I am finally free!!!! ..."

Forgiving "him" doesn't mean that I have forgotten about the abuse endured. Forgiveness means I chose to reclaim the power that God has for my life. In changing my mindset, I stopped holding onto the bondage that God wanted to release and be used for his glory. However, I was unable to tell if he read any of them since we were not "friends".

I have allowed God to release the chains of bondage associated with the pain, shame, guilt, and feelings of unworthiness that attempted to keep me within its grasp for the rest of my life. I now truly see myself as God does. I realize that I am worth more than the world's finest jewels and will not accept being treated as anything less by anyone else ever again. I shall continue to share my testimony to inspire others in finding their voice through God and be set free.

INTERNAL REFLECTION QUESTIONS:

What past hurts are you holding on to that are keeping you from being your best self? How have these issues (or events) affected your relationships?

_____

_____

_____

_____

_____

By forgiving that person, do you feel like you are condoning their past or current actions towards you? List the reasons that you feel this way.

_____

_____

_____

_____

_____

Do you understand that even without an apology, your forgiveness helps to strengthen and heal you in your brokenness? If not, list the reasons that you feel this is impossible and allow God to do the POSSIBLE in your life.
Matthew 19:26 KJV

_____

_____

_____

_____

_____

MY APOLOGY TO ME AWAKENED ME

By: Dr. J. Le'Ray

*L*ove (for others and self) is an essential component of life and affects the matriculation process. As a child, love is felt in a plethora of ways from a variety of people or the lack thereof.

"One can only give what they received", is what my Mama shared with me at the age of about 29. I am still processing this statement and seeing how it played a huge part in my life, my spiritual maturity, my perception of me, and an awakening to divine truth.

Mama was a loving and nurturing Soul to any and every one, whereas Daddy was on a path of seeking love. Daddy was the oldest of his siblings and the only "stepchild". Needless to say, this status caused him a lot of pain that he harbored internally. These circumstances manifested into some glaring attributes that affected each of his children, and, for me, played a huge part in my earlier life decisions and spiritual slumber.

Being the third "living" child, and the second daughter to be birthed from Mama and Daddy's union, life was interesting. From the age of three, trauma was a norm in my life. The pain that Daddy carried was nursed by drugs, alcohol, and women. This caused a cycle of trauma that impacted my psyche for quite some time; which in turn, equated to a continuous cycle of slumber spiritually and warped my perception of me.

The first traumatic memory I have is being put into a car abruptly and Mama speeding out of our community, also referred to as "The Projects", as we were chased and being shot at…by my Daddy. Was this what love was? This could not be life. My slumber was steadily being intensified with my trauma induced environment. BUT GOD!

Life continued and so did the housing transitions, drama, trauma, and a "different type of love". This "different type of love" was shaping the "me" I had to deal with over many years. We moved quite a bit, living in almost every Project in my small rural North Carolina town. Each move brought about another layer of trauma.

As life progressed, so did my toxic ways of coping, toxic mechanisms of defense, lack of self-love, and my spiritual slumber. Daddy's way of "loving" me led me to often wonder why he didn't love me, why he didn't take the time up with me and the question lingered…what was wrong with me? Not only was I going deep into a spiritual slumber, while attending church every Wednesday and Sunday, the toxicity from my wounded Soul was intensifying and manifesting in negative ways internally as well as externally.

As a teenager, I ate my way through many things and became morbidly obese. Obesity was another layer of trauma. Being ostracized, teased and stereotyped morphed into an insecure, aggressive, male attention-seeking adolescent. Becoming the bully was how I coped with the negative reactions (and out of control emotions) received from becoming morbidly obese, sexually abused and feeling unloved. I was truly lost with very low self-esteem.

I was angry and did not understand why my life was so different from those who surrounded me. My Spirit was certainly sleepwalking in a physical vessel created for a divine purpose. It was like a normalized daze…year after year…even while attending church several times a week.

I was angry at myself often for making decisions that left me filling empty. In this phase of being lost and not knowing who I was, the spiral continued and the layers kept piling up. I continued eating, being promiscuous, seeking male attention, and making sure I hurt you before you hurt me.

I continued the journey and continued making the same type of decisions. Who was I? Why didn't I fit in? Why? Why? Why? I was always questioning my existence as it just seemed as though I was always out of place. My spiritual slumber was such a weight due to my lack of knowledge and truth about who and whose I was.

Well, the teenage years came and I was still seeking love in all the wrong places. I was introduced to a young man in prison through a family member at the age of 15. Writing letters and receiving letters became the highlight of my life.

Letter after letter soon moved to phone call after phone call. I had a boyfriend (who was in prison hours away). He loved me, he made me feel like I had never felt before. That love I was seeking from Daddy, I suppose. We wrote and talked all through his "bid". He got out and I was so happy, but he was two hours away. That did not stop a thing. Was I awakening? It sure felt like it.

My best friend and I conjured up a good story to tell her parents about an educational trip planned for a town two hours away. They were staunch supporters of education and any ask concerning education always got us a YES. Yep, it was the town where my boyfriend lived. I actually told my parents the truth and they allowed me to go without questioning me. This was normal as they trusted me and had no idea that I was "messing around".

We made the trip and stayed at a hotel with my "boyfriend" and his cousin. We thought we were grown for real. My boyfriend and I had sex (I had no idea what I was doing) and after he climaxed, he said, "You are pregnant". I heard him and did not think twice about it. I was 16 years old and thought everything about this was fun, cute and grow-upish. My spiritual slumber was not as heavy in this season as I thought I was "in love". The attention of this man was masking my true state of being.

About eight weeks later I became sick and had a slight idea as to what was going on. Remember, he told me I was pregnant. My Mama was in Germany visiting my eldest brother who was in the Air Force and my Daddy was doing what he did (work, alcohol, drugs, and women). My sister-in-law, and best friend, got the hunch that I was pregnant and thought it best that I go take a test at a nonprofit organization who worked with teenage mothers.

I remember that morning like it was yesterday, I was terrified and did not know what to expect. We arrived at the center, I took the test, and I was pregnant. I gave birth to my only child 10 months later, missed my high school graduation, (I did not get to walk with my classmates and receive my honors) and cried like a baby. I vowed then that I would never miss another graduation.

By the way, how in the world was I a mother and had never

had an orgasm? Yep, that is just how "green" and inexperienced I was but was trying to be grown. The sleepwalking had only gotten a bit more complex while I journeyed still in a deep state of spiritual slumber.

Mama and my family stepped in like a champ. I was able to go to college and graduate with honors. This phase was filled with cycles of drama and layers of trauma as well. BUT GOD! Daddy and his "vices" escalated causing a level of stress unbearable for me; being that my mother, sister, and son seemed to be in danger.

They moved to the city I was in about 2 hours from our hometown and we continued the journey. I made it through and started teaching third grade immediately after graduation. I was still in a spiritual slumber, lost, insecure and using the aforementioned vices and defense mechanisms to soothe my pain and bring clarity to my confusion….so I thought.

The first year of teaching was HELL! Literally, I was one of two Black teachers in an affluent elementary school with about 2% of minority students. I was not good enough for these parents children, let them tell it, and I had to work 20 times harder than the other first-year teachers in the building because of who I was and what I looked like. I cried every day I left that building. This certainly was not what I signed up for…this could not be what teaching was all about!

Upon leaving the school building on October 31, 1997, I traveled with my Mama to Washington, DC to see my eldest brother who was very ill. On the trip back, I was grading math papers (I was teaching about graphs) and began feeling bad. I stopped grading, laid my seat back to take a nap as Mama continued the drive back down 95 South.

I was awakened to my Mama yelling and crying, blood shooting out of the middle of my face, and an army of paramedics around me. All I heard was, "What is your name? When is your birthday? What day is it? How old are you?" The paramedics were constantly suctioning the blood from my throat as it was flowing like a fountain. Then I heard them say that the "Jaws of Life" were needed to cut me out of the van.

The process happened, I was rescued and put on the stretcher, then put into the ambulance for transport to the hospital. I distinctly remember the paramedics continuing to suction the blood from my throat area, yet it was becoming very difficult to breathe. I took the suction device from them and began navigating the device in the places that allowed me to continue breathing…THAT WAS GOD!

After emergency nose reconstruction and a 10-day hospital stay, I was released and began the recovery process. I was still in a spiritual slumber, lost, insecure and seeking male attention. Recovery continued for two years. In the midst of recovery, we moved back to that small rural town in North Carolina where it all began.

I gained employment, at the middle school in which I attended, and was matched with my 7th grade Math teacher as my mentor. This changed the game for me and shifted my perspectives and mindsets in regards to education. I was in it, after many thoughts of leaving. I remained in public education as a classroom teacher for 17 years and currently serve as an advocate in a myriad of ways.

This move back home was great and allowed me to become a bit more grounded. I began awakening with small moves forward, yet I was still seeking that "love" from a male. I continued eating and being promiscuous as I dealt with not knowing who I was, what I was called to do and being just plain insecure. I was a naïve and vulnerable woman and the enemy capitalized on that.

I met "Beelzebub" himself through the same family member that I met my "prison boyfriend turned baby daddy". When I tell you, I went on a spiritual ride from one realm to the next and one level to the next. I was diagnosed with Kidney cancer and had to have a left nephrectomy. I was truly lost, but in the midst of it all, I began to be found through constant seeking, praying, praising and worshipping. The tremendous amount of hurt, pain, abuse and being used matured me and prepared me for the journey ahead. I made a power move with "Beelzebub" and my son that landed us in Atlanta, Georgia. Through the pain, I was awakening. I was being shaken by Abba Father himself.

The "ATL" was a different animal, but my current "boyfriend" had prepared me very well to navigate the many games and manipulation tactics. He was a master, to say the least. We lasted every bit of three months in our new state until all HELL broke loose. It was in this space and place that I began to cry out to Yahweh all the more.

I was a single mother, to an eight-year-old son, in Atlanta with a boyfriend who did not have my best interest at hand. This season of life took me to some dark places mentally, spiritually, and physically. I was vacillating between slumber and "the awakening". I was angry with myself, out of touch with myself, and often wondered why I was doing what I was doing time and time again. It seemed that I was stuck in a vicious cycle that looked and felt like self-sabotage.

In the midst of a break-up, my "boyfriend" was ordered to leave by the court system. He literally took all of my clothes, one shoe from each pair of my shoes, broke up all of my elephant collection and curio cabinet, took all of my jewelry, my required medicines, and all of my sorority keepsakes from my collegiate activities.

I hid out for about 2 months, sent my son to NC to live with my Mama temporarily and even stayed out of work. I was devastated, scared, lost, ashamed, and filled with more doubt than ever.

I received a call from the school district's Human Resource department that gave me an ultimatum; come back to work or resign. Talk about the bounce-back season, I snapped back and began to press forward on the journey again. I came out of hiding, moved back to my apartment, got my son back to Atlanta and began to get back to a regular routine of life.

The next few years were filled with increased eating, promiscuity, and unhealthy relationships. All the while, I continued to seek Abba Father's face all the more. It seemed the more I got hurt and taken advantage of, the more I sought after Him for solace, peace, and understanding. It took a few more rounds of "boyfriends" and trying relationships before the cycle ceased.

I taught full time, finished my masters, and dually enrolled in two separate Universities to complete my doctoral studies in Educational Leadership & Administration; I also got my certification add-on for educational leadership. The spiritual slumber was shifting to a journey of spiritual awakening.

All the while, I was an emotional mess, gorge eating was a

normal activity and I was becoming more and more obese. Once again, I moved another "boyfriend" in my house. Still seeking that love I craved as a little girl and thinking that all the drama and trauma I witnessed was just how it was supposed to be.

Can you say another level of drama and trauma? This was an anointed vessel with some vices that had him bound. My, my, my…what a ride? This one involved theft from my son, theft of my car, stalking, and plain intimidation to the third degree. The shift in my spiritual state was surely my saving grace during this season. In the midst of this relationship, my emotional gorge eating resulted in a weight gain up to 485 pounds. Life had gotten really difficult physically. My current school situation was a nightmare, yet I was continuing to seek Abba Father's face and praying for guidance.

These prayers resulted in gastric bypass surgery in 2010, my boyfriend leaving me for other women and me beginning the journey of finding my authentic self; through the hell at work and in my personal life. Yep, my spiritual awakening had leveled up through much pain. In this season I was also attuning more to who I was. I identified that I had to apologize to myself as well as forgive myself for all that I allowed to happen to me by being a willing participant.

The journey was so very difficult, but oh so strengthening. The Word truly became the light unto my path. I was awakening to who and whose I was daily. I had always read the bible, but I was truly understanding it and my Spirit was being fed and strengthened daily. The layering and leveling were truly ascending me to higher heights with The Lord at an accelerated rate. I accepted my apology to myself and steadily went deeper into a relationship with Abba Father. Accepting my apology to myself served as a catalyst for me to continue the ascension process without being a constant hindrance to the process.

In August 2010, my husband found me. Glory, Hallelujah for that! He was LOVE in the flesh and consistent across the board with every Soul he encountered. I had never experienced such Agape Love. Abba Father continued to reveal me to me and joined us as one through Holy Matrimony. We began our journey as one and the layering and leveling continued. We were growing and ascending together. Our Souls were awakening all the more.

I am wide awake and pressing with a full throttle now as a limitless Spirit on a journey; totally submitted and committed to Abba Father's will and way. My journey was necessary, my pain was necessary, it all made me who I am today. Through all the gifts Abba Father so graciously bestowed upon each of us, I now am able to: boldly and confidently lead national educational programs, birth a business (and build it as the CEO), become a bestselling published author, serve as a strategist for national initiatives, unite, and help others as we advance the Kingdom all for His glory!

I am an awakened Soul for Abba Father and Abba Father alone. I now know who I am and whose I am. This is all the love I need to journey forth, on purpose, shining bright, just as He ordained for me before He sent me to this realm. My apology to me awakened me! As I continue this journey, my daily mantra is: Die flesh, Die!!! Rise Holy Spirit, Rise!!!™ This keeps me grounded and keeps that messy, ugly flesh in check. Join me in speaking this mantra to yourself as you press forward shining bright as an Awakened Disciple!

INTERNAL REFLECTION QUESTIONS:

Have you ever apologized to yourself? If so, what brought you to apologize to you? If not, do you see the necessity in doing so after reading this story?

_____

_____

_____

_____

_____

We know that forgiveness heals. Can you forgive yourself without apologizing to yourself?

_____

_____

_____

_____

_____

Has apology been a factor in any other relationships in your life? Did the apology positively shift you and the relationship involved?

_____

_____

_____

_____

_____

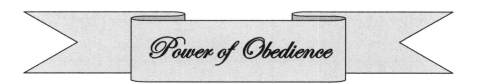

Power of Obedience

By: Patsy Clowney Bloom & Verganell Thomas Craig

bedience is the key to salvation. Obedience is defined as compliance with an order, request, law or submission to another's authority.

Biblical obedience to God means to hear, trust, submit, and surrender to God and His word. *"If you love me, keep my commandments."* Obeying God is like building a house on a strong solid foundation that stands firm when storms come. *"To obey is better than sacrifice"* is repeated numerous places in the Bible. Being religious (going to church, serving on committees, giving to charity) is not enough if we do not act out of devotion and obedience to God.

We fall short of our blessings by not being obedient. Obedience requires one to move self out of the way, allowing the Holy Spirit to lead and guide. The key to obedience is submission to God.

SCRIPTURE REFERENCES

Ephesians 6:5-9, Isaiah 1:9, I Samuel 15:22

MY BRIDGE BETWEEN HEARING AND ADHERING

By: Durcus Hiller

mbedded in the Scripture, 1 Samuel 15:22, is the passage *"obedience is better than sacrifice."* I learned and memorized that passage as a child. I knew it by heart. In fact, as a youngster, adolescent, young adult, and as a full-fledged adult, I would mouth the words as I heard my mother in a cadent voice recite the five words, *"obedience is better than sacrifice"*, as a reminder to me. Throughout my growth and development, physically, mentally, and spiritually, that five-word phrase was my constant personal reminder. The phrase shaped and cultivated the person I would become.

Over a span of almost five decades, I formed and lived a misconception of what "obedience to the Lord" really meant. Somehow, I fashioned, in my mind, that the act of obedience was likened to an artful game of darts. While the objective in the game of darts is to aim and shoot for the bullseye in the center of the dartboard; one could still score and accumulate points by hitting any one of the outer rings. Outer rings had point values, too. If the dart landed anywhere on the actual board, and not on the surrounding wall where the board hung, it was still good and had some value.

There was nothing that occurred in my life that indicated what I believed was not so. Understandably flawed, and very much human, my targets were almost hitting the target or missing it. In my life application, I believed that if I hit anywhere near the bullseye of what the Lord asked me to do, I would be in good standing with Him.

In 2009, I received a new target from the Lord. From the onset of hearing what He expected of me, I knew it was going to be problematic. This target was so different from anything I ever had to do. His calling, at that stage late in my life, was to be a public-school system teacher. The process of hitting that target, in lieu of the individual I had become, had no outer rings. It meant enrolling in a college or university; staying and being present on the journey to obtain the necessary credentials to teach, as well as changing careers. There were no outer rings involved along the continuum of any of those phases of the target. After several unsuccessful negotiation sessions with the Lord, I yielded.

After being accepted at Mercer University, I was on a schedule to hit my bullseye. My expected graduation date was May 14, 2011. While in attendance as a night student, I decided to obtain an additional degree, concurrently. Pursuing two degrees, at the same, would only push my completion date further to August 2011. In my mind, I justified that three extra months to a purpose that took five decades to actualize would double in benefit. My modified target was not discussed with the Lord. Unaware of the magnitude of my creation of outer rings surrounding the target I was given, I took aim.

While aiming high, my new target required more of my time. Therefore, I resigned from my employment and attended school full-time. As I gained academic momentum, the vicissitudes of life happened - an entangled cord of death, grief, and sorrow tied up every aspect of my being. Key people in my life unexpectedly expired: my husband, June 2010; my step-father, February 2011; and my beloved mother, May 26, 2011. There was no way that I could finish school. At the time of my mother's death, I had two courses left. The most painful part of those two remaining courses was that they were required because of my decision to seek another degree.

All the education classes and electives were successfully and scholarly satisfied. However, my will and way of creating outer rings held my education degree in limbo. The university informed me that I had to complete both the Information Systems and the Education degree programs since I'd declared both majors. Not realizing the full scope of my dilemma, I shut down, refused to finish school, and blamed the Lord for taking the people that I dearly loved away at a pinnacle time. Those same people were the cheerleaders that supported and encouraged me when I faced big and small obstacles in life. They guided and counseled my flailing and failing aim in just about every major target I attempted as an adult.

In a fit of rage, a stupor of anger and defiance, I doubled down and announced to my sons that I could not go on. Finishing school was not in my sights. They too were grieving. Nevertheless, they reminded me of my target and the need to finish regardless of what I was feeling. What I had poured into them over the years began spilling out. My oldest son, David, asked me *"What is God saying?"* My second son, Johnathan, reminded me that I had to finish knowing it would have made his nana proud. He said, *"Madre, we don't quit!"* My third and fourth sons, Stephen and Michael-James, reminded me that it was all in

His plan. Thank God for my sons. They presented valid arguments and I valued each one.

I went to the Lord with blame and a barrage of questions of why's and how comes. If obedience is better than sacrifice, why was He requiring me to sacrifice so much? After all, I was being obedient. Daily, I sought Him with my accusations and feelings of abandonment. Yet, I heard nothing. Since my adult sons were holding my feet to fire encouraging me to finish school, I did so. Both degrees are dated August 13, 2011. The achievement paled in comparison to the pain I suffered and shouldered. Still, the Lord was silent regardless of my pleas for His accountability in my devastation.

For the next four months, September through December, I felt the absence of the Lord. The intensity of the void overrode any feeling I had ever experienced. Isolated and left to myself, I was emptied and more aware of a state of nothingness. I felt cut off from God. I had no measure of sadness or even grief. Like a robot equipped to perform a set amount of programmed functions, I managed to do day to day things.

I forced myself to feed my chihuahua but resented having to do that. Helen, now a dear friend, gifted the dog to me when my husband died. Imagine being responsible for something that was a constant reminder that you were left alone. Navigating through the day was a daily target. Each day, my dart hit the surrounding wall, nowhere near an outer rings. The days, weeks, and months seemed like emotionally and hopefully bankrupt moments in time. The New Year had come, and I expected nothing new.

January 6th was my mother's birthday. Early that morning I wept and longed for the agony of the valley that engulfed me to be no more. While uncontrollably sobbing, I heard a voice anew; not to be misconstrued by a new voice. I knew for a fact that it was the Lord. But there was something noticeably different. His voice was more audible than I had ever experienced. On other occasions, He would lovingly and gently nudge me toward a target via my coaches and support system. Now, He was emphatic and demanding as He voiced, *"obedience is better than sacrifice!"* Then, He continued, *"apply for the teaching position"*.

A teaching position was so far from my mind. Where had the Lord been all this time? For every tear I had cried, I had a question for Him. However, my questions seemed unimportant to the Lord. He appeared fixated on my applying for a job. Therefore, I looked for science teacher vacancies on all the public-school district websites in the Metro Atlanta area. There was one vacancy. My cohorts in education had been looking for teaching positions but to no avail. God had me apply for the one position in the middle of a school year. Completing the online application for that one position seemed endless and useless.

Sometimes positions are filled but the human resource department has not closed the posting. Knowing that I called the school and asked if the job had been filled. The woman that answered the phone stated, *"today is the last day we are accepting resumes. Would you like the fax number?"* Startled by her response, I scrambled for something to write the number down. One of the requirements for my education portfolio was to complete a resume. After adding completion dates and degree information I faxed the document. January 6th was a Friday. I received a call to come for an interview on January 9th. After the interview, I knew my chance of getting the job was slim.

January 19th I was asked to come in for the second interview. They asked me to prepare a lesson to teach students. I created a standard-driven lesson fused with the use of 21st Century technology. However, the classroom was not equipped with working technology and the students were administrators acting like adolescents at the peak of puberty. It was a setup. Honestly, I do not remember how I did. I do remember how I felt when they told me they would let me know their decision.

The call came the very next day. They offered me the job. I was processed on January 26th. My first official day of teaching middle school science was January 27, 2012. I have been teaching ever since. Things changed in many ways as I aimed for those outer rings.

Still hitting and missing, the shift in my mindset did not occur until recently. January 2019, seven years later, I learned what my five-word mantra really meant. The teacher was schooled on "obedience is better than sacrifice". The Lord made me aware that my aim was always off because I did not understand the contrast presented. The phrase was comparing **"obedience"** to **"sacrifice"**. Going back and reading the passage in context, I was sorely amazed. Saul was directed by God to annihilate his enemy and to not keep any of the spoils. Saul disobeyed God. Whatever he thought was worth something, he brought it back and offered the spoils to God as a sacrifice.

God viewed Saul's disobedience as sin. His offerings were not even recognized by God as having any value. My mindset shifted because my focus shifted. The application was only doable by understanding what I knew. Up to this point, every target I had nonchalantly aimed for and hit the outer rings was my rendition of what I wanted God to have. For my own convenience, I'd revised the target and reduced it to sacrifice. Contrary to what He asked of me, my sacrifice had no value.

Late in life, but never too late, I learned that the opposite of obedience was rebellion. Since the shift, my aim has greatly improved. Most importantly, I have learned that obedience is my bridge between hearing and adhering to what the Lord wants of me.

INTERNAL REFLECTION QUESTIONS:

In what ways have you given the Lord what you wanted Him to have instead of what He asked for?

_____

_____

_____

_____

_____

Sometimes what we render (or give) to Him defers, defeats, or defects an outcome. How has what you rendered to the Lord impacted you today?

_____

_____

_____

_____

_____

Knowing your costs, what advice would you give to another now?

_____

_____

_____

_____

_____

WHEN GOD SAYS DO IT

By Jennifer JJ Jones

I've heard the line that dogs are "man's best friend" but never really thought much of it. Who would have thought that the dog that I rescued from death, God would use to save my life? That morning on June 25, 2013, at 3:00 am I was awakened by a beating sound against my nightstand. Chester, my dog, loved to sleep under his favorite blanket and he was hitting his head on the nightstand trying to get under the blanket. After five or six tries, I decided to help him out. I reached over to grab the blanket on the floor and rolled right over a lump in my breast. I immediately sat up and in a calm but somewhat alarming voice and said, *"I have a lump in my breast."*

I woke my husband and repeated those words to him *"I have a lump in my breast."* and took his hand and rubbed it under my right breast. My husband then told me not to get alarmed; but that I should have it checked out in the morning. I really can't remember what I thought, but a calm came over me and I went back to sleep.

A few hours later, I was up and preparing to go to work with nothing on my mind except calling my radiologist to find out when I could come in. I remembered that I had another doctor's appointment that Friday morning at 9:00 am for my shoulder that had been bothering me, but that was the least of my worries at that moment. I arrived at work at my usual 7:30 am time to gather my thoughts. I knew my doctor's office probably wouldn't be open until 9:00 am and I began to get anxious.

I could hear God telling me to calm down. I don't think I was as anxious about the lump I had discovered as I was about my husband being unphased by the news. The more I thought about my husband not volunteering to come with me, the more I became angry.

On a whim, I decided to go ahead and call my radiologist office. To my surprise, someone answered. I went into my spiel, *"Good morning, my name is Jennifer Jones and this morning I discovered a lump in my breast, and I want to come in and have it checked out."* The person told me that I would need a referral from my primary physician before I could come in. She went on to tell me what needed to happen and gave me the fax number for the office. At that moment my heart went down to my feet. Again, I could hear the Lord telling me to calm down and to focus on Him. I ignored His voice and continued to think this thing out for myself.

What would be my next move I wondered to myself? I knew I would never get my primary physician on the phone. Just as I had that thought, I remembered that I had spoken with her nurse practitioner and she had been very helpful. I still had her number, so I called it and, of course, they were not scheduled to open until 9:00 am; it was just 8:30 am. I left her a long message explaining my discovery as well as what was needed to see my radiologist. Finally, by 8:50 am, I had an appointment for 10:00 am.

Once I had the appointment, I called my husband and asked him to meet me at the doctor's office. In my head, I was going through all sorts of scenarios, not of my condition, but how I would give my husband a piece of my mind. I was upset that he had not called me to find out what was going on and that had to call him.

I arrived at the radiologist before my husband. As soon as I walked in the door, the nurse said *"Mrs. Jones, follow me"* and I did. As I was going in my husband walked through the door and I told him that I was going in the back. He didn't offer to come with me, so I went ahead.

I love my radiologist because she is a believer and knows the power of God and was not afraid to talk about it. She did a sonogram on me. As she was completing the procedure she told me that she wasn't going to sugar coat things. I told her that I wanted it straight. She went on to tell me that she would not know for certain until she did a biopsy, but she was pretty sure it was cancer. She went on to give me some instructions on what I need to do to get the biopsy scheduled and what to expect. I took it all in and the Lord, once again, told me to be calm.

After I got dressed I went into the waiting area. My husband was on the phone totally distracted. After some time he finally realized I was there. I told him what the doctor said. To be honest, I was still upset from his lack of concern earlier and did not pay much attention to how he responded. He walked me to my car and I don't know what I wanted him to say or do, but I didn't like his lack of "MY kind of response." I think in his way he was trying to comfort me, but I was not focusing on what he was trying to do I was focused on what I thought I wanted him to do.

After he walked me to my car, he got into his car and I just sat there. After a few minutes, I just began to cry. I don't even know why I was crying. He saw that I was not driving off, so he came and pulled up beside me. He asked me what was wrong, and I yelled at him, *"what do you think is wrong, I HAVE CANCER!"* In my head I was thinking, you idiot, what kind of question was that, is that all you got. Just as that thought rolled off my brain, it hit me, the Lord told me to be calm, and suddenly I knew why. He revealed to me in that instance that this was going to be hard for my husband and that even though I was going to go through this journey I had to be calm - that calm was for my husband.

God wanted me to listen to Him and depend on Him and not to do anything out of His will. In Isaiah 41:13 it says, *"For I am the Lord our God who takes hold of your right hand and says to you, Do not fear; I will help you"*. He wanted me to be obedient, and through my obedience God was going to work on and with my husband. In Deuteronomy 5:33 it states to *"Walk in obedience to all that the Lord your God has commanded you, so that you may live and prosper and prolong your days in the land that you will possess"*. Through the Holy Spirit, God provided me with everything I would need to comfort and keep me through this. All He was commanding me to do was to be obedient.

I had to have 7 chemo treatments and my husband only came to the first one with me. I had 34 rounds of radiation and my husband did not come to any of those. It was hard for me not to get into my feelings and let my husband know what I was feeling, but God told me to be still. God led me to what I began to call my theme song through my journey, *"I'm in the midst of it all"*, by Fred Hammond. I played that song morning, noon, and night to remind me that God is always there no matter what. I had to be obedient by keeping still and listening to God.

God told me that I was not a victim, but a VICTOR. I was never afraid and never asked "why me". After following God's instructions, I began to thank God for entrusting me with this testimony. God allows things in your life that sometimes are not for you but for other people. It may be for those whom you are close to or even for people you do not know. I now know that God was working on my husband, and I had to be obedient to God so that He could do that work.

Fast forward, after 4 years 5 months cancer free, I went in for my 6-month check-up on December 19, 2017, and my radiologist found another mass in the very same breast. After doing a biopsy I found out on December 22, 2017, the day before my birthday, that the mass was cancerous. So, my journey began again, but this time, my husband never left my side. He was there every step of the way and continues to be there. God knows what He is doing, and He never has to tell me twice. I know that God not only wants me to be obedient, but He wants me to depend on Him. He is awesome.

INTERNAL REFLECTIONS QUESTIONS:

How does God speak to you?

_____

_____

_____

_____

_____

When has God told you to do one thing and you did something totally different?

_____

_____

_____

_____

_____

What is your life like when you are obedient to God?

_____

_____

_____

_____

_____

LEARNING THROUGH THE GROWING PAINS OF OBEDIENCE

By: Crystal C. Cruse

The general concept of obedience both in the Old and New Testaments relate to hearing, hearkening, or submitting to a higher authority.

If I had to sit and think of the first time that I can remember hearing God's voice; it would have to be when I was just a young girl, maybe between the ages of 8 and 10. As the church service was approaching the end, the preacher finished his message and asked if anyone needed prayer. He directed those in need to come to the altar.

This Sunday my mom went to the altar. This was nothing new at all. However, this particular day, when the preacher said Amen, I could hear my mom's voice. She had always had the gift of speaking in tongues, but I had never witnessed it. I just heard the tales of her going into "the spirit" and speaking in another language.

My mom's voice quickly changed into a voice my ears had never heard. I stood there staring at my mom in shock. Mainly because her voice was so deep and raspy like a man, and then I did not hear the spiritual language. What I heard was a deep raspy voice saying "I AM THE GREAT I AM, I AM THE RULER, I AM THE GREAT I AM, THIS IS MY HOUSE!!!!" The first time that it came through clear I thought that maybe I was just hearing "voices." After hearing the same sentence three times, I started to get scared because the voice was getting deeper.

I quickly gathered my things and stepped out into the vestibule of the church with the rest of the children. When I first stepped out there, I was going to tell them what I heard, but they were already out there clowning *"Crystal I didn't know your mom could talk in Spanish."* Oh, they laughed and laughed. I replied; *"It is not Spanish. She is speaking in the spiritual tongues."* The rest of the children who were in the vestibule looked at me and said I mean your last name is a "Mexican" name.

The adults started to come out and I was anxiously waiting on my mom because I was ready to go. I later shared with my mom what I heard while she was speaking in the spirit and at that point, I learned that everyone does not have the same gift; but when God blesses you with a gift you have to use it. My mom went on to tell me if I ever get blessed with that again that I should listen carefully because the message could have been for somebody else at the church.

As a young child, I absolutely loved the church. Every time the car cranked up and I knew that we were going to church, I was right there. This included Sunday school, bible studies, and two choir rehearsals a week. My mom taught us, as children, that all things are possible through Christ who strengths us. This was my life until I became a teenager maybe 12 - 14-years-old.

I started to meet new friends between school and visiting other churches. I would go spend the night with my new friends that I'd met, and I saw that you can do as you please Monday to Saturday as long as you were in church on Sunday. During these impressionable teenage years, while out playing with friends, I saw local drug dealers serving or "selling" to the Deacons and Trustees *(of the local churches)*. Sometimes I would see them come with no money and offer favors. I would even witness them stumbling out of the local liquor houses, but when Sunday came they would be right there holding their "positions" and "titles" in the church.

After a few months passed, I began to question exactly how loyal did I have to be in the church? I can hear God telling me *"Stand Still"*, I just couldn't understand how "Deacon A" and "Trustee B" could get to be so phony and fake and still continue to come in Sundays, lead devotions, and take up the offerings! Sure, I heard the father telling me, *"their battle is not yours,"* but I still found myself worried about 'Deacon A' and 'Trustee B.' In my worries, God told me *"you are not going to the church for man!"* Despite that, I was still questioning exactly how 'Christian' you had to be Christian? So, I figured I would go about 60% Christian and 40% street. I felt as though I was in a pretty good ratio considering I did not have any rank in the church.

While living my best 40% street life, my mom and God continued to sit me down and keep me out of harm's way. I heard nothing! I was "good". Then the unthinkable happened — I got pregnant! The man who would be the father of my child, was just a "friend". That friendship quickly came to a halt when I told him I was pregnant.

Now pregnant at 20 years old, the man that was my best friend was not my friend anymore, and I had turned my back on everything else that I knew. What was I supposed to do with a baby? How would I make it as a single mother? He already had six children. Lord, what am I going to do?

I had a whole life growing inside of me, out of wedlock; I was scared, nervous, and felt alone. So, I did the only thing that I had been taught to do when your back is against the wall and you feel all odds are against you —I began to Pray and I prayed and prayed and prayed and prayed.

I took my broken heart and my lost soul back to church, and that was where I found peace for those remaining months. God knows I'm so glad that I was obedient. I gave birth to my son on February 28, 2003; a beautiful healthy boy and he was blessed. The week that we were released from the hospital my sons guardian angel sought him out; to pray protection over my son, to break "generational curses" and to cover my son from any harm. There were a few other things that I didn't quite understand but when I went over them with my mother she knew exactly that the prayer was necessary and ordained. I am confident that my son's blessings and covering manifested only because of OBEDIENCE.

Moving forward, I'm living with my mom carefree, bill free, kind of kid-free. I mean, I had no responsibilities really; I worked and used my money as I pleased. From the ages 21-28 I was my son's babysitter while my mom worked 12 hours and served as "mom" to him and me. I had a few jobs in between those years and didn't think about saving a dollar because I was where I'd planned on being; right there with my mom.

Then the unthinkable started to happen, out of the blue my mom started to have plans on her days off that had nothing to do with my son. I was either paying someone to keep him or I was staying at home. Sitting at home just wasn't an option at the time. Then there were days that my mom stopped coming home and started to go on vacations.

A few weeks later, I got to meet the man who had stolen my security blanket. Yes, I was angry – livid, actually. It was such a drastic change that happened so quickly. Don't get me wrong, I was happy to see my mommy happy; but I wasn't used to what was going on and the responsibilities of being a full-time parent.

A month or two down the road, my mom calls all us, her four children, to tell us that her boyfriend had proposed and that she would be planning her dream wedding. Ooh Joy, oh joy! I was so happy for my mother, until the reality of her getting married started to set in and I started to think and process what was occurring.

Did that mean that she and her husband are going to move into the house? What was going to change? My mind was on one hundred but no one brought it up so I didn't bring it up. I continued to live carefree as though there was no change to come.

Then, the day came. I received a text message from my mom, *"where are you? I need to talk to you."* I waited a while and text her back that I was on my way to the country. "The country" was how we referred to our home. I pulled up and she was already there with her overnight bag packed waiting on me. Here came the conversation that I was not ready for, but it had to be had. I had six months to find a job and find a home for me and my son.

The panic was on. I went and applied for a very low-income apartment that was within 25 miles of where I stayed, but there were no list shorter than two years. While in the middle of all of this I found out that I was pregnant with my second child. Yet

again in a similar situation as before. *"Why Lord? Lord have mercy —
why? I prayed every night! I go to church when I wake up on time! Why am I
being punished?"* This time it was way more disheartening because
there were two "possibilities" for the father.

At this time in my life, I was the "Christian" that knew the
bible verse that would justify the wrongs and turn them into rights
in my eyes. For example - Exodus 21:23-25 *"But if there is harm,
then you shall pay life for life, eye for eye, tooth for tooth, hand for hand, stripe
for stripe."* I told myself that I was in the situation because I had
one man that I was "friends" with, but he was such a cheater so
instead of cutting him off, I simply cheated back.

When I told him I was expecting, he immediately said *"I don't
want no more kids right now; I'm not ready. I just had my son!"* He did
not know that I had been unfaithful and he asked me to have an
abortion. The second 'friend' had no children and he was more
than happy to be a dad. But he was in a relationship and I really
didn't want the drama of dealing with his girlfriend; or with my
"main" friend, as I affectionately called him. While all of this was
going on, I still couldn't understand, why me. I was just in a
whirlwind of feelings coupled with being overwhelmed trying to
find somewhere to stay.

In the middle of this storm, I was completely lost. My
emotions turned into rage. My rage turned into anger and my
anger started to turn into disrespect. I was so angry and hurt at
that time that I forgot where and who my strength comes from! I
ran around for weeks like a chicken with my head cut off. I just
could not come to grips with all of it.

I heard God speak in a faraway faint voice *"you are stronger than
this, You have to REACH DOWN AND GRAB THAT*

MUSTARD SEED FAITH, AND MOVE ALL THESE MOUNTAINS!" I began to pray, and I prayed, and I prayed. All I knew, was if I had to go stay with someone, I was willing to do what I had to do.

God speaks, *"Giving up is never an option, it's okay to reach out for help. Be steadfast and get up. You may get tired, but YOU NEVER GIVE UP!"* The next morning, I woke up refreshed with a new attitude. Knowing that I needed to lean on God and that my family would never turn their backs on me.

I reached out to my siblings to fill them in on everything that was going on. My eldest brother and his husband were there within two weeks, riding around the city looking for a place for me, my son, and my unborn daughter. Thank God for OBEDIENCE. I found peace daily in keeping in my heart and declaring with my mouth, *"God grant me the serenity to accept the things I cannot change; courage to change the things I can; and wisdom to know the difference."*

I gave birth to my daughter at the end of March. She was a beautiful baby and absolutely perfect. I also had a tubal ligation. However, after the six to eight weeks from having my cesarean section and tubal ligation, I started to have a lot of menstrual complications. Between March and June of that year, I was having my "lady friend" every week (sometimes I would get two weeks off). I was so tired and weak all the time; so I finally made an appointment with my OB-GYN. Once I explained what was going on, she had me come in within that week.

I was so nervous as I was waiting for the doctor to come back in the room. When he entered, he started to tell me that I would need to have a partial hysterectomy. However, he recommended a full one because there could be a recurring issue considering I was 29 and I had two children. The doctor went on to tell me that once I have the surgery that I would be on bed rest for six weeks. He further educated me on how serious the procedure would be. I told the doctor that I have a six-month-old daughter and an eight-year-old son. I was confused about how I was supposed to just take six weeks off from life as a single mother. I told the doctor that I will need some time to figure some things out.

I contacted my family to let them know what was going on; and started trying to arrange things so that I could get back to the doctor and make the appointment. In that same moment, my mom called me back and told me that she had spoken with her husband and that I should just let her know the dates and she was going to come for the six weeks —BUT GOD! This was, by far, never what I expected with her being newly married, but I truly appreciated my mother and all of the sacrifices that she made for me and my children.

September 25, 2011, was the day I was scheduled for my surgery. My mom and her husband arrived at my house early and we left for the hospital. Everything was perfect and, by the grace of God, I came out without any complications. My mom stayed right by my side for the six weeks and made sure that my two babies were good and that I was too.

While being on bed rest I had a lot of time to reflect on life and choices that I had made in the past. I started to wonder week after week – *"where were all 'my friends', 'my ride or dies', 'my homies'?"* Oh, man, were my feelings hurt. I lashed out on social media, pouted, gossiped, but I should have been thanking God; because that was the beginning of my mindset shift. In regards to my response and reaction to what I deemed "not right," leading to choices aligned to disobedience! You see, these types of blessings are rare. While reflecting I was forced to count my many blessings, big and small, and appreciate the genuine things I had in my life. I'm glad that my mom is my mom and she is always obedient.

Obedience has been a major key and resolution to all main parts of my life. I feel as though obedience, faith, and humility all go hand and hand; and with all three you can make it out of any situation. I am still in the midst of growing, learning, and maturing spiritually daily. I am grateful that I can continue to do all things through Christ. I pray that everyone who takes the time to read my story will be encouraged! #UPRAY4MEIPRAY4U

INTERNAL REFLECTION QUESTIONS:

Can you identify moments in your life that caused stress, pain, or hurt because of your disobedience?

_____

_____

_____

_____

_____

Have you caused stress, pain, or hurt in someone else's life because of your disobedience?

_____

_____

_____

_____

_____

Moving forward in life, will your mindset shift result in making wiser choices?

_____

_____

_____

_____

_____

Power of Faith

By: *Patsy Clowney Bloom & Verganell Thomas Craig*

F aith is defined as a complete trust or confidence in someone or something; a strong belief in God or in the doctrines of a religion, based on spiritual apprehension rather than proof. "Now faith is the substance of things hoped for, the evidence of things not seen" (Hebrew 11:1).

Faith combines assurance and anticipation based on past experiences that God's new and fresh surprises will surely be ours. Two words describe our faith: confidence and certainty. Faith begins by us believing in God's character — that He is who He says. The endpoint believes in God's promises —He will do what He says. Without faith it is impossible to please God.

Our faith is forever leveling up through the life experiences Abba Father ordained for us to encounter. It is important to know and understand that faith is not based on what our natural eyes see; yet on what our innermost being knows. This assurance and certainty is amplified as our relationship with Abba Father is deepened. It is in the moments when what we "see" in the natural makes absolutely no sense. It is also in these moments that we must press forward with a blind and radical faith. Shifting our mindsets to know that everything is already done and all experiences strengthen us as we journey.

SCRIPTURE REFERENCES

Ephesians 2:8-9, Corinthians 5:7, Corinthians 2:5,

Matthew 21:22, Romans 10:17

THE PATHWAY OF FAITH

Dr. Crystal Cooper

"For I know the plans I have for you declares the lord, plans to prosper you and not to harm you, plans to give you hope and a future." **-Jeremiah 29:11**

Melody Beattie says, "Faith is like a muscle. It must be exercised to grow strong. Repeated experiences of having to trust what we can't see and repeated experiences of learning to trust that things will work out are what make our faith muscles grow strong".

As a child of God, we are not exempt from failures, fears, and disappointments. Oftentimes, when we feel that we have an unanswered prayer, we must persevere and build our faith in hopes that it will multiply exponentially; to soothe the gaps that various moments in our lives offer. My stories are some of many different exercises in building endurance in faith. My stories are the inner workings of, "remaining faithful when no one's looking, enduring pain when the room is empty and like standing alone when you're misunderstood." (Charles Swindoll)

As I write this, I am in the last stages of a divorce, building faith in career advancement, and worried about the health of my aging parents. Through it all, my faith is what sustains me; knowing that God sees me, hears me, and knows what I need. I have allowed the foundation of God's purpose in my life, which I learned as a young child, to constantly strengthen my faith that I continue to lean on as an adult.

I grew up in a small suburban town near a large city in New Jersey. Born an only child of my parents with two older brothers from my dad, I had a normal upbringing; with many opportunities that would prove to mold and fine tune my life. My mother, the first of ten children, was a high school teacher. My dad, the first of three, worked in IT, was a master sergeant, and a disc jockey. The worldview that I was offered inside the home was nurturing and supportive. Many who viewed my life from afar, would have thought that I had the world and, in many cases, I did. However, I struggled internally with my own identity, academic challenges, and the desire to maintain quality friendships as an only child.

I lived on a long street divided by single family homes and multi-family homes. I attended six schools before high school; one in kindergarten, one for 1st- 5th grade, and three different schools for 6th -8th grade. This experience all had its ups and downs. Overall, I needed faith to end and begin new school experiences every year amidst such change. The school moves were attributed to high tuition and environments that didn't fit well behaviorally and academically for me to be able to learn and grow, as my parents expected and hoped. I take full ownership of these experiences, because I had a difficult time learning how to fit in at public schools as compared to smaller private schools. These experiences were all influential in my upbringing, in cultivating stronger relationships and stronger conflict resolution among peers.

I was often teased by my peers for being conceited, and for living a lavish life-style. We were your typical middle class family, but my parents made sure that all of my needs were met. Extra-curricular activities always added to my weekly routine. My mom was a high school English teacher and had high hopes for me and my future. Though difficult to comprehend, the negative side of my living experiences was influential in me building faith among the most difficult situations. As I was given various experiences to use my talents of singing, dancing, and acting through the years, I continued to cultivate leadership experiences through elementary school. Allowing God to mold me even as a young child. Faith in God's work for my life took me from experience to experience, not knowing that I was being built for many more positive opportunities in my life.

In 6th grade, I had the most difficult time getting along with others. I was bullied, and taunted the entire year; I even got suspended for the first time for fighting. I would hide under the steps during lunch because I didn't want to face the "giants" who would wait to verbally or physically harm me at lunch. What was sad about this was that I kept this secret for years from my parents, until my early 20s, feeling too heartbroken to reveal the inner pain and fear that I felt at that time.

They never knew why I lost over 30 pounds that year. My teacher never even noticed my absence from the line. I would drop off when they left and drop back in when I heard them coming. That time under the stairs is very vivid to me today. It was the time that God was revealing to me my purpose and strength in my quietest and loneliest times. Though an 11-year-old girl, I know now that God was giving me these faith moments to build a stronger foundation for what was to come in my life. He was teaching me that I didn't have to hide any longer during adversity, but to stand in the midst of it with unyielding faith.

The additional trials that would come, didn't excuse me from my calling or purpose, but they provided me the opportunity to endure to the end. As a young child, I didn't realize that everything was unfolding and that perseverance and trust in God would help me evolve.

After attending the three different middle schools, I landed at a Catholic high school; where I still struggled with friendships, fights, and participation in what we called "girl drama." Though a challenging time for me, I continued to move forward academically and became involved with clubs and opportunities that would prepare me for faith building experiences. Through the negative perception that I'd built, my teachers still instilled faith in my abilities to successfully complete my assignment of graduating and moving on to college.

I applied to many different colleges and received letters of non-acceptance. Thinking that a historically black college (HBCU) was for me, I realized that God had a different experience in store for my life. I landed at a demographically diverse college that would serve to help me soar through many challenges and experiences. I wasn't accepted as many others were, but one school took a chance to accept me while I took remedial math classes. As the non-acceptance letters came in, I continued to have faith that I would be a college graduate, and my story continued to unfold for God's glory.

As I matriculated through school, I began to participate in many leadership opportunities that would mold my life. God allowed me to become a resident assistant, president of different civic organizations, a member of a prestigious sorority, treasurer of the student government, and the 1997 Homecoming queen. Through all of my positions and responsibilities, I took a chance to use my faith in God for Him to see me through. My last fight was in college, although I lost my position as a resident assistant, God hid me in it all to become the treasurer of the student government. The student body had faith in my abilities, despite my poor decisions, and voted me to represent them. Faith won! Grace won!

One of the most memorable experiences for me was climbing towards success throughout my educational profession. When I realized that I desired to become a teacher, I felt that it would be a simple task. However, becoming certified was not as easy as I thought. I realized I wanted to be a teacher after losing the desire for fashion merchandising, though I worked part-time in retail for several years. Once I had a firm foundation, and the plan to support children, I matriculated through school to obtain my bachelors in education. Many didn't know that I'd failed at the National Teachers Exam two times, making the third time a success. Faith was with me every time.

As I started to teach, I learned from how to lead and grow from my colleagues. Amidst small conflicts with colleagues at this large, urban, Title I school; I maintained strong relationships with my supervisors who believed in me and afforded me many opportunities to lead. I was also asked to become a certified presenter with an international consulting organization, which I still am dedicated to today. This work aids in me providing professional learning to educators all around the world in social and emotional learning practices. The faith that my principals and mentors had in me, led me to be able to travel the world and meet people who have helped build my character. My purpose was to help children have greater school experiences, where they were able to take risks, learn how to belong, feel significant, and enjoy learning. Things I lacked my entire school career. I continued to keep my faith in my abilities. After 6 years in education, I worked successfully for the state as a reading coach, in a one year sabbatical teaching position. All of these experiences earned me the title of Teacher of the Year. But GOD! After working as a teacher, mentor, and leader, I desired a change. The many rewarding leadership experiences allowed me to move forward by becoming a literacy leader when I moved to Georgia in 2005.

God can use even the ashes from our worst choices in life and transform them into something good.

I moved to Georgia to be closer to my parents who moved there two years prior. The move was based on several factors that were both positive and negative. I wanted to experience a new position in education, and I knew Georgia could provide more opportunities for me. However, what made the move more necessary was an experience that I would soon never forget.

I experienced a major church hurt that was public and damaging to my personal reputation and faith in God. Though I own my part in the story, it didn't help that it afforded me the loss of relationships and the positive reputation that I worked hard to build for so long. Unfortunately, my faith In God declined because I never thought that He would allow me to hurt publicly. Or take away my leadership role and ability to sing his praises as a member and leader of the church choir and the praise and worship team.

As I moved from the church to try to find another, I was lost, lonely, and confused. I thought that God had forgotten me and didn't care about my future. How could he push me away and make me out to be a bottom feeder in The Most High church?

This was one of the most hurtful experiences in my life. So much so that today, 14 years later, it still riddles my soul. In the middle of this devastating experience, my car was repossessed and I truly felt that I was at a place of no return. Due to my parents being the most caring and loving individuals, they were able to purchase me an even nicer car the very next day. The amazing part of this story was that they were visiting from Georgia on the very Sunday that the car was removed from my driveway. God knew what was going to happen, but he shielded me from any more embarrassment and allowed me to be elevated amidst difficult circumstances. God loves us so much that, even when we fail, He will shield us and yield us to a better life in Him. Our name is VICTORY!

Though I'd forgiven all involved, including myself, I lost a lot. It took me years to forgive and accept the demotion that God allowed, but my faith in a positive life ahead continued to surround me. What we must always do is to empathize with those who also are hurt by our actions and always stay focused on never making the same mistakes again. Which I am proud to say, I never did. This mistake was costly, but I still desired to stay close to God, become a faith leader, and an example of God's grace. Though I never sang again, I danced on a dance team at church and volunteered in different ways. Jesus couldn't get to the cross without Judas, so I realized that even the people who betray you or hurt you are part of the plan. As Psalm 119:2 says, "Blessed and favored by God are those who keep his testimonies, and who consistently seek him and long for him with all their heart."

Once I moved to Georgia, I attended a job fair. While I met with different districts, my mother was at work too. With my mother's assistance, she walked around and spoke on behalf of my abilities, one person she spoke with was impressed by my resume. I know, what you're thinking, but my mother was the catalyst to my turnover. She ended up meeting someone who allowed me to be hired on the same day. Prayer and God's intercession afforded me great opportunities, just from my mother's encounter. Several successful and challenging experiences ensued while I worked as this school. However, we were able to successfully transform a school's academic progress, which was a rewarding experience for myself and the students. I desired to go back to school for my Master's degree at a prestigious college. Once I got accepted I began to take courses, with no specific major. Though I took leadership courses, I was not properly accepted into the leadership program. Once I saw positive movement in the course, I applied and was denied. If it weren't for the faith of the advisor, I may not have been as successful as I am today. I successfully graduated in 2007 and also became an assistant principal, amidst many who didn't believe in my abilities to be a strong school leader. Again, my supervisor saw and knew my potential and helped me gain that amazing position. God places people in your life for a purpose. She was sent by God for me.

God continued to give me signs that I needed to continue to pursue additional schooling. I successfully completed the program two years later, moved to obtain a Specialist's degree in 2011, became a principal, and finally earned a Doctoral degree in 2018. At present, I am the only one in my family with a doctoral degree and it is an accomplishment that I never knew would be part of my destiny. Throughout each of these experiences, I did it without a strong academic test score. I did have people who believed in me and also had faith in my abilities however. I have found that not only do you need to build faith in yourself, but you also need to surround yourself with people who have faith in you. Gratefully, God afforded me loving friendships in my adult life that offered me the ability to be supported and sustained through all of my challenges.

I learned more about myself as I grew older and that was that I needed, to know "thyself." Once I was given an opportunity to learn my strengths, I was able to see more of why I had a deeper faith. Taking the Strengthsfinder® assessment, I learned that I earned the qualities of being strong in modeling these five strength characteristics: Positivity, Learner, Communication, Responsibility, Achiever.

The fact that God equipped me with these leadership qualities, enabled me to utilize my strengths through many faith-building experiences. I joined a new church where I also learned that I had four major spiritual gifts after taking the Network® Assessment. God endowed mercy, intercession, leadership, administration, and faith in me, I was astounded that I was gifted these strengths all along.

I believe that knowing your strengths allows you to leverage a higher calling in all you do. Once you focus on your strengths, they will catapult you into understanding God's calling on your life. With my leadership and spiritual gifts, I understood why God chose me to be a leader in education and gave me the opportunity to experience some of the most difficult challenges. I realized that He had also blessed me with the gift of FAITH. What an astounding revelation!

Just one month after I decided to divorce my husband, my mother had a mild stroke yet through it all, I kept the faith. I continued to thank God for letting my mother survive something that could have killed her or alter her way of life. Today, she is walking and talking without assistance. Although she is dealing with the first stages of dementia, she is able to function positively with God's protection and healing powers.

Faith is built through experience and as believers, we must not only strive to persevere through the adversities, conflicts, and disappointments; but we must be steadfast in knowing that God has a plan for it all. It may be ugly, embarrassing, or even public, however, in due season, God will raise you up to be a leader despite what it looks like.. The pathway isn't always straight. It could be narrow, wide, hidden or long. Either way, we must be vigilant to face our difficulties with faith that God will see us through it all. I am always reminded, that however things turn out to be, God is in control. Things will work out for our good. Trials come to make you strong and I can attest that the strength that follows takes you to the next trial with more power and purpose.

God always does more today than he did yesterday. He desires our obedience, trust, and faith in HIS abilities to do what He ordained and planned for our lives. There were moments, when I wanted to give up and give in, but God said in his word in Isaiah 14:27, "For the Lord of hosts has purposed, and who can annul it? And His hand is stretched out, and who can turn it back?"

God's purpose over our lives is to be a living testimony so that we can share with others how His word lives and breathes in us. We are not to grow weary in well doing, but be a model and example of God's grace over our lives. No one said that it would be easy, but I am firm believer that faith is the ONLY pathway to endure life's challenges. Rejoice at all times and show God that you have unwavering faith in him to see you through. God wants us to trust him heartily from our souls, to speak life, glorify, and honor him with praise. God grants us power over all things and creates opportunities for us to apply that power throughout our lives. We must use this faith to allow God's presence to manifest itself in all areas of our lives.

We are called to believe in him, trust in his works, and sustain faith in ourselves that our purpose in life will be revealed for his glory in Christ Jesus. Do not lose heart or give up when it seems like God has forgotten about you, or passed you over. I am a witness that he hasn't. Delay is not denial, and wait is not never. I am a walking testimony that God is ALWAYS on time. Forgive, love, and allow God to use you for HIS glory. Continue to allow God to mold your character and build you to be better every day. Words are powerful and the power of life and death is in the power of the tongue. So pray, speak faith in all your interactions, and trust God to fulfill his promises. Not only does love conquer all, but having faith a as small as a mustard seed will be all you need. Submit to the leadership of the Holy Spirit with faith, and God's unconditional love, in the name of Jesus.

INTERNAL REFLECTION QUESTIONS:

When you face trials and challenges, how do you input a faith-minded belief system into your daily walk?

_____

_____

_____

_____

_____

What areas of your life do you need to apply more faith in order to draw closer to God's purpose in your life?

_____

_____

_____

_____

_____

How can you utilize your own testimony to garner strength in orders to employ more faith?

_____

_____

_____

_____

_____

THE PRODUCT OF A TOTAL WOMAN

By: Tracy D. Vault

*M*y journey began June of 2005 when I found out that I had fibroids. They were surgically removed; however, in July of 2007, they grew back, and I had to go through a total hysterectomy.

In June of 2005, I went in to see my gynecologist for my yearly checkup. As always I was a little nervous, because there is something about being at an hospital that makes me unsettled. I waited to be called to the examining room. Once there I changed my clothes to put on the gown that they had already laid out for me.

My doctor and the nurse were rapidly getting things ready. I approached the table to prepare for my checkup which involved a routine pap smear to check for cervical cancer or any other abnormalities. During that time I was talking and laughing to help ease the nervousness. As I laid there, and the doctor began to check me; she also began talking to me. She continued talking but this time it was not with me, but with the nurse. I knew something was not right.

I was 36 years old scared and inquisitive about what they were talking about. I knew that it wasn't good after the nurse left the examining room and upon returning, she had another tube in her hand that was used to store a second specimen in for testing. My doctor began wrapping things up and in the process, she began speaking to me again. She began telling me that after examining me she can positively confirm that she felt several fibroids, one was the size of a small watermelon. I was in disbelief because I did not understand how something so big could store itself in the human body without my stomach bulging out to make me look pregnant or like I was carrying a tumor.

I had no knowledge of having fibroids and neither did I have knowledge of where they came from or what they were doing to my health. My doctor explained to me, as she handed me a brochure, what I needed to eat and drink to keep the fibroids from possibly getting bigger. Because of the size and seriousness of my fibroids I was scheduled to come back to the doctor in two weeks to discuss the results of my pap smears.

I went home and googled the word fibroid because I wanted to become as educated as possible on what was happening to me. I also needed to know my options of treatments. Not that I did not trust my doctor, but I wanted to be prepared knowing that I would receive the best options for my health as well as my well-being.

My life had changed in one day with the news of my fibroids. In researching I became familiar with the four different types of fibroids —intramural, subserosal, sumucosal, and pedunculated; the most common one being the intramural fibroid.

Two weeks passed and I went back to my doctor for my follow up and to discuss what would happen next. My doctor explained to me that my pap smears were negative for cancer. However, the fibroids were too big to treat with any other medication. I needed surgery to remove them. She also explained to me in detail the type of surgery I would be having, a Myomectomy.

The news of not having cervical cancer was a breath of fresh air. I was worried for the entire two weeks waiting for my results. During my consultation, I listened carefully to my doctor as she explained the surgery procedure. She also explained that the type of fibroids I was carrying were intramural fibroids. The thought of me having fibroids growing inside of me and one being the size of a small watermelon really grossed me out, but I knew I would be much better after the fibroids were removed.

During the entire time of my waiting period for my surgery day, I kept the faith, I continued to pray the prayer from Psalms 118:17 *"I shall not die, but live, and declare the works of God."* Being that the only time I was hospitalized was when I gave birth to my son, learning that I needed to stay 24 to 48 hours in the hospital was unsettling. Yet, through it all I continued to pray that God would ease my stress and make sure my surgery was a success.

The day before my surgery, my mom, dad, and aunt arrived just in time for my pre operation appointment. The night before my surgery I did everything that was ordered for me to do. I laid in bed and I said my prayers. I also read a scripture that I depended on so much, Isaiah 41:10, *"So do not fear, for I am with you; do not be dismayed, for I am your God. I will strengthen you and help you; I will uphold you with my righteous right hand."*

The day of my myomectomy surgery we left the house and arrived at the hospital early. My wait time in the lobby was very short. I had become a little leery and scared but I remembered the scripture that I had read the night before. As they wheeled me to the operating room, I talked the entire way. They lifted me to put me on the operating table and all I remember from there is counting backwards from 10.

During recovery I was a little drowsy from the medicine and my throat was sore from the tube that they'd put down my throat. I didn't experience any pain until I was in my private room. I was awake and doing well. My surgery was successful. All of the fibroids were gone, and I was as comfortable as if I was at home.

To my surprise two years later in 2007 I was diagnosed with fibroids again. This time I had become angry and disappointed. How could this be happening to me all over again and so quickly? I gathered myself and prepared for the unknown of what I was going through. I still had faith because, just like God brought me through my first surgery, he would bring me through again. I was not going to let anger, sadness, or bitterness be a part of my journey.

No research this time because I remembered everything from my first round of fibroid surgery. Before anything could be done my doctor wanted me to complete another consultation. This time I waived the consultation and asked my doctor if she would just give me my options since I had already been examined and diagnosed. She went on to tell me that my best option would be to have a total hysterectomy due to the fibroids coming back and that there were more this time.

I asked my doctor if she would give me some time to think about what she'd said. I wasn't sure if I was ready for the option of having a total hysterectomy. All I knew was, I had to seek God for confirmation. Hebrews 11:6 states, *"But without faith it is impossible to please him: for he that cometh to God must believe that he is, and that he is a rewarder of them that diligently seek him."*

My surgery was scheduled for July 5, 2007. I contemplated canceling my surgery several times after hearing all the horrible events and stories that women were experiencing after having a total hysterectomy. The hot flashes, weight gain, and low sex drive all brought me some concern. Nevertheless, I thought long and hard about my option and decided that a total hysterectomy would be the best for me. I felt a little out of place because I didn't know any women my age that had ever had a hysterectomy. The only thing that crossed my mind was not ever being able to bare children. I immediately thanked God for the son he had already blessed me with.

My condition was really bad, but after my hysterectomy I would not have to deal with any of the pain, heavy bleeding, anemia, or bloating that usually came with having fibroids. My family was with me just as they were during my first surgery. The day before my surgery I talked to them and said that I was not afraid and everything was going to be just fine. My surgery was scheduled for 7:30 am.

We arrived at the hospital and upon arrival my doctor spoke to me to explain how the surgery would go. Since I waived my consultation she wanted me to know where all the incisions would be made. Minutes after speaking with my doctor it was time for me to take that walk to where I would prepare for my hysterectomy. I entered the room, changed into the hospital gown and minutes later they were putting the IV in my hand. There was no time being wasted.

I was taken to the operating room and lifted from my bed onto the operating table where my hysterectomy would take place. I remember talking to the anesthesiologist, but our conversation was cut short, before she asked me to count from 10 backwards. I was out.

When I woke up, I was in the recovery room. I felt bummed but I was so blessed that God had brought me through one more time. Before being wheeled to my room my doctor wanted to share the pictures of my uterus and the fibroids that she had taken out. I was grossed out but I was so happy that I made the decision to have the hysterectomy.

My surgery was a success and I was blessed to leave the hospital two days after with no complication. No more fear of cervical cancer, fibroids, heavy bleeding, anemia or bloating. I did not mind the hot flashes and I can proudly say that my doctor never prescribed me any medication per my request.

In closing, my hard decisions turned into the best decisions that I've ever had to make. I am a woman that had a total hysterectomy and I feel good. The spiritual outcome of my experience is that God wanted me to have faith, no matter what my body had gone through.

Through divine intervention God assured me that I am the same woman that He created me to be, even after my hysterectomy. We all go through things because God did not create anyone to be perfect. There are many things that may cross our pathways. Whether it's high blood pressure, diabetes, heart disease or a hysterectomy we have to keep striving Him; things like these do not exempt us from a good life or the love of God.

No matter what my health had taken me through, I stood on faith, knowing that God would deliver me. Trusting God, faithfulness, and peace is what I consume in my life, and I encourage you to do the same, regardless of what had been removed from me.

INTERNAL REFLECTION QUESTIONS:

Have you ever asked God why were you chosen to be one that had to endure with the agony of having to live with the unknown?

_____

_____

_____

_____

_____

How will/ have you rebuild/ rebuilt your life after you have been broken and feeling like what you have gone through has held you in bondage?

_____

_____

_____

_____

_____

Do you trust God enough to know that he is there to help you restore your faith even through times that you felt like giving up?

_____

_____

_____

_____

_____

GRIEF: THE LONELY ROAD TRAVELED

By: Temeka Miller Thomas

I cannot breathe. My heart has definitely stopped, if not but for a fleeting moment. My feet feel as if they have been weighed down by cast iron. I cannot move, yet I can actually see myself running down the hall screaming for this not to be true. Is this what it feels like to have an out of body experience? People are screaming my name and telling me to breathe and to stop running, yet I do not tarry. I must get to his bedside. I must hold his hand. I must hug him close one more time. I must stare at his face and see my own staring back at me just one more time. I've got to tell my best friend not to go.

I suddenly hear my own voice screaming from my soul, *"Don't go daddy! I'm coming! Baby girl is coming!"* Just a few more steps before I reach the door and prove to everyone that my beloved father would not leave without saying goodbye - no - he would wait on me. I reach the room and he is laying there, so still with a faint trace of a smile on his face. It is true, what **someone** told me in the parking lot is true. He is gone, to return to me no more. As my feet left the floor and blackness engulfed me, the last thing I remember before fainting is thinking to myself that my life will never be the same.

To say that my father and I were close is an enormous understatement. It's as if our souls were connected, we could finish each other's sentences. My father stood 6'2 with broad shoulders. I remember as a child, in elementary school, I would be so happy when he picked me up from school. I wanted everyone to see how big and strong my daddy was.

He was a man's man in every sense of the word. He was my protector. He loved me regardless of my mistakes. He often neglected himself, so that I could have what I needed. Whenever I had a bad day, all I had to do was hear his voice and everything would be okay.

So, at the age of 43, there I was, feeling like a helpless child with a broken heart. The God that I was taught to love had taken my father away and I was mad at him and at the world. I told myself that I could not wallow in self-pity, for my mother was still living and I had to be strong for her and take care of her. I could use the energy that I was feeding my grief with to be there for her. After all, she was the one that lost her **partner** of 46 years. She had lost her husband that always took care of her. Yes! That's what I'll do. I'll make sure she has what she needs. I got the opportunity to do just that for only 7 short months, as she left this world just 7 months after my father.

At my mother's funeral, I was beyond numb. I sat there like a zombie. I could tell that both my mind and body were on the verge of a complete meltdown. I tried to go back to work a few days after the funeral. I was sitting at my desk and then all of a sudden, a rush of grief engulfed my whole being. I was consumed to the point that I was rushed out of the department and found myself sitting in HR having a full-blown panic attack. My doctor removed me from work for several months. It was during this time of quiet and solitude that I had to face my fears, acknowledge my present situation, and have some long one on one talks with God about my diminishing faith.

I did not have faith in myself, in God, in my family, or in the comforts of this world. There was nothing or no one that could comfort me. I laid in bed for hours and days at a time in a severe state of depression.

Then, one day I heard someone humming the beautiful words of an old gospel song. That, someone, was me. In all honesty, I tried to fight it! I was actually mad at myself. I did not want any connection to anything spiritual. I just wanted God to come and take me as well, and yet, here I was singing His praises. Little by little and slowly each day I would push myself out of bed. I'd say things like, *"Ok God, if you still hear me help me get out bed and experience some kind of joy today."*

I remember one day, I finally surrendered and fell to my knees in my bathroom at home. I couldn't do this anymore by myself. The only thing that I knew was that regardless of the situation; I still had a God that I could call on. Here I am mourning my parents—the same people that loved and worshipped this same God! What did I have to lose?

He'd been faithful to me before. He'd showed up in my life and rescued me many times before. His Word was still the Word and great was *STILL* His faithfulness! I laid on the floor and wept for what felt like hours. Bible verses started rushing through my mind like a flood. That's when I remembered that, although my faith had diminished, if I could just muster up about a mustard seed's worth of faith, God would meet me at my faith level!

For days and weeks to come, I kept praying, not to feel better, but for my faith to come back. I longed to have that reassurance back in my life. No matter how hard the winds blew, or how many traps the devil set for me, my faith in our omnipresent God would hold my feet planted firmly on His word. Through prayer and searching the scriptures, I ran across two familiar passages of scripture. Psalm 34:17-18 and Psalm 27:13-14 both stuck out like a sore thumb. These scriptures declare:

The righteous cry out, and the LORD hears them; he delivers them from all their troubles The LORD is close to the brokenhearted and saves those who are crushed in spirit. brokenhearted and saves those who are crushed in spirit. - **Psalm 34:17-18**

I remain confident of this: I will see the goodness of the LORD in the land of the living. Wait for the LORD; be strong and take heart and wait for the LORD. - **Psalm 27: 13-14**

What a mighty God we serve! No matter what you face in life, don't ever lose your faith in God. I began to recite these two scriptures at every turn. There were so many days that my tears were more prevalent than my smiles, but through my tears, I recited God's word back to Him. I told Him that He *"hears my cries"* and. *"because I'm crying out to You, Your word says You will deliver me! You word says You are close to me and my broken heart and spirit!"* I told God that only because I know He heard me and no one else. I was confident that I'd see His goodness again on this Earth!

I didn't have to wait until I get to heaven to feel His presence. I knew that I was a recipient of His grace and mercy each and every day. And, because of His goodness and His grace I'd wait for Him patiently at every crossroads in my life. Not only would I wait, but I'd wait with a heart of expectancy and a spirit of gratitude through my faith in Him.

As I come to the close of penning this brief overview of my power of faith in God, I want to encourage you. There is nothing God will not see you through. Your test may be different from mine. Perhaps you are not facing grief, but other things in your life such as divorce, the loss of a job, the loss of your home or finances, feelings of despair or depression, or maybe feelings of hopelessness. No matter what you are currently facing, or will face in the days to come, I want you to be encouraged and know that God will never leave your side.

Take small steps to regain your faith. No matter what it looks like or what it feels like; you will get through your storm. Just remember that every storm runs out of the rain, and there's never been a storm that has caught God by surprise. Beloved, rest in the sweet bosom of God. For it is in His presence that you will find every answer that you need. May the peace of God be your portion now and forever.

INTERNAL REFLECTIONS QUESTIONS:

How can you strengthen your faith?

_____

_____

_____

_____

_____

Has God EVER failed me in the past?

_____

_____

_____

_____

_____

_____

Is there anything that is too difficult for God?

_____

_____

_____

_____

_____

STRONG FAITH AS A YOUNGSTER

By: Marvin Craig

My friends were going missing. I wasn't sure what was going on. The faces changed often. Some stayed longer than others, but I was there every day. The hospital waiting room and family areas were filled with children's laughter and noise one day as we played with trucks, sirens, and other toys; then the next day, it was quiet with a solemn somber from grief. This was my life cycle for about three years.

When I was four years old, I was diagnosed with lymphoma cancer. At the time I was living in a small rural town in Alabama. The care I needed was not available in my city. My Mama was a mighty praying and faithful woman of God and interceded on my behalf while advocating for my healthcare. After a few weeks, my doctors worked it out for me to get treatment at the Children's Hospital in Birmingham, Alabama. This hospital is about two hours from my hometown. That's where the faith got stronger.

I started my treatment at the Children's Hospital which called for me to stay for a few months. I met children there with the same cancer. We used to play one day and the next day they would have passed away. I would ask my mom what happened to my friend. She would tell me *"God had better plans for them."* I would

COMPILED BY DR. J. LE'RAY

cry and mom would start to pray with me.

The bed next to me would soon be filled again with a roommate to play and laugh with daily. Not too many days later, the same thing would happen again… and again. It was like a routine. I was a four-year-old child witnessing the death of so many children from lymphoma, leukemia, and other kinds of cancers. It was hard and scary at times, but my mother always told me, *"God knows what's best for you and I know everything will be alright."* Her blind and radical faith was covering, encouraging, and inspiring to me.

After being in the hospital for about three months of treatment, the doctor came to my room and said *"I have some good news… you can go home!"* My mom immediately started to praise God. We went home for a short spell. My release was a blessing and posed another dilemma where faith was the pilot. My treatment regimen required me to go to the Children's Hospital in Birmingham every two weeks for a while. The treatment frequency decreased over time form once a month, to once every three months, to every six months, and then to once a year for about four years.

This was on top of my Mom being a mother to three other children (I was the baby boy); being a wife and working a full-time job. Faith was everything during those long arduous years of treatment. All I had was God, my mom, and father. My father had to stay back and take care of my other two brothers and sister, and of course he worked to keep the house going while me and mom traveled back and forth between Meridian and Birmingham.

My mom was so tired with all the traveling back and forth. One day, while we were on our way back from treatment, she said, *"I am so sleepy."* At the age of 10, I said to her, *"Mom, I can drive."* She agreed and proceeded to give me instructions. She said, *"Stay in the right lane and wake me up in York, Alabama."* I prayed the whole way and asked God to guide the wheel. I was driving, full of faith, on Interstate 20 at 10 years old. Mom was resting so peacefully when I got to York, that I decided to just take it on in.

When my mom woke up we were pulling in the yard at home. She said, *"Boy you didn't wake me up."* I told her that since she was sleeping so peacefully I decided to go all the way. I told her that I wanted her to rest and that, *"I knew that God had me."* I was a happy little boy when I drove my mom home. I knew about the power of prayer and faith at a very young age. I knew that God could fix anything. Eventually, the treatments were done and God had manifested divine healing for me.

As I got older, I started to do what Marvin wanted to do. I had not forgotten what God had done for me. I just got off course with a corrupt and stifling mindset. I had a lot of ups and downs; including back to back incidents of getting in trouble at an early age. I wanted to fit in with the crowd. In hindsight, the crowd was good, no troubles, no charges, no stress and not worried about me. I got caught up in a cycle of unproductive decisions that landed me in a situation in which my freedom was in the hands of "a system". I had to do the time because I did the crime.

Right before this cycle of bad decisions, tragedy slapped me in my face. I walked into my father's house and found him dead. I was in the eleventh grade and this changed my life tremendously. Where was my faith? I was rebellious, angry, lost, and confused; nobody could tell me anything.

My father was my ace boon coon, my best friend, and my confidant. He taught me how to be a real man, how to drive (at an early age), how to use a chain saw, how to survive, and how to take care of the family. I saw him go through and survive many trials and tribulations. He faced all of those giants and kept going.

After my season of selfishness and doing what Marvin wanted to do I, once again, had to have stronger faith knowing God would deliver me from the situation I'd created from my decisions. Thank God for mercy and grace. Guess what He did… Just what he said! I was a free man with a renewed mindset and a faith that had been strengthened through my past experiences.

In July of 2010, I made a faith move. I moved to the metro Atlanta area. This transition was purposeful; I was praying and believing for a wife. After all of my bad decisions and selfishness, God brought me my beautiful wife. My whole life shifted for the good. I am a testament that Proverbs 18:22 is a living Word, *"He who finds a wife finds a good thing, and obtains favor from the Lord"*. We united and began our journey.

Our faith carried us through a few things and then God moved in a miraculous way. An assignment was awaiting my wife and I (we are one) in Washington, D.C. Another test of faith was upon me. My wife, that God brought to me, had to move to Washington, D.C. by herself for about six months. That was the hardest, most challenging period; having to be without my wife for six months. Faith and obedience certainly guided me through that strengthening season.

In January 2015, God moved again, and I finally moved to D.C. to be reunited with my wife. I was so happy. I packed up the house and hit the road. We settled into our little home and it took me about two months to find employment. I started working in a field that I was very passionate about and was blessed to work for two and a half years finishing concrete.

It was on March 3, 2016, that that job came to a halt because I was in a traffic accident leaving work. I was sideswiped and pushed into a curb by a semi-truck that came into my lane. The injuries caused me to have surgery and various therapies for over a year. Faith and obedience guided my path once again.

I could not work, finances were challenged, and we were functioning with one car. I had to take my wife to work, come back to our community, and go to therapy three times per week. It was hard, but God.

In March 2017, just as my therapy was coming to an end, I started having problems with my right eye. I went to the eye doctor and he immediately advised me to go have an MRI of my head. I followed his recommendation and the MRI revealed that I had a tumor (meningioma) sitting behind my right eye in the eye cavity. This tumor was causing my eye to look different from the left one.

This started a series of opinions; choosing a doctor, choosing a treatment path, deciding on a radiation location, and then 31 days of radiation treatment. My wife and I prayed about it and journeyed through each day. During these thirty-one days of radiation, I prayed and gave it to God. He told me that He was my everything and I just had to let Him be that.

When I started my treatments it was weird, but I had been through this before and I knew my God had already fixed the problem. My body went through many changes. I lost my appetite, my smell, I slept a lot, I was seeing double for a minute, and had mood swings. But God. I just stayed prayed up, as always. I tell people that there is nothing too hard for God.

Even though I can't go back to doing the job I love, I'll just do what God blesses me with. I thank God for giving me the ability to do more than one job.

As you read, faith has power and every season of my life challenged my faith and shifted my mindset to know that God is in total control. I want to thank GOD, once again, for giving me the strength to keep going. I also want to thank Him for blessing me with a wonderful wife that did not give up on me in the midst of each of these tests. She walked every step of the way with me and is still walking.

Sometimes I wonder where I would be without a mindset shift to obey and have steadfast faith in God. Now, I'm blessed with four granddaughters that bring us so much joy. I want to spend as much time as I can with them and teach them about faith, obedience, and the true love of God. I need them to know that they should not depend on man, but God, and to always let their yes be yes and their no be no.

Lastly, I would like to tell them and all who read this story:

Don't be a people pleaser.
Don't follow the crowd (You can enter God's Kingdom only through the narrow gate. The highway to hell is broad, and its gate is wide for the many who choose that way. Matthew 7:13).
Before every decision say to yourself, *"What Would God do?"*
Know that God sees everything.
Faith up and keep pressing.

As Jesus told the Disciples in Matthew 17: 20, *"You don't have enough faith. I tell you the truth, if you had faith even as small as a mustard seed, you could say to this mountain, 'Move from here to there', and it would move. Nothing would be impossible".*

INTERNAL REFLECTION QUESTIONS:

How does faith affect your life?

_____

_____

_____

_____

_____

What moments test your faith?

_____

_____

_____

_____

_____

What will you do to continue shifting your faith?

_____

_____

_____

_____

_____

REFERENCES

Scriptures used were retrieved from www.biblegateway.com and www.biblestudytool.com in the following versions: New International Version (NIV), New Living Translation (NLT), Good News Translation (GNT, and New King James Version (NKJV)

10 Myths about Hysterectomies Women can safely Ignore. (2019, March 5). Retrieved from Readers Digest: rd.com

Types of Fibroids (2019, March 5). Retrieved from webmd.com

ABOUT THE AUTHORS

JENNIFER (JJ) JONES
Author, Educator, Inspirational Speaker

Jennifer M. Jones, known by most as JJ, is the Executive Director of Student Development at Southern Methodist University where she has been employed for the over 30 years. Sixteen of those years in various positions within Residence Life and Student Housing. She received both her BA in Sociology and Masters of Liberal Arts from Southern Methodist University.

In various capacities, Ms. Jones has given workshops on college campuses across the country. She is the 33rd National President of the National Pan-Hellenic Council. She served as the President of the NPHC for 10 years and Vice President for 4. She is currently working as the Program Lead for the Black Greek Letter Consortium for the All of Us Research Program. She serves on the board for the LeaderShape Institute, and is co-chair for the NASPA Fraternity and Sorority Knowledge Community. She is a member of the Kappa Zeta Chapter of Zeta Phi Beta Sorority and has been a member of Zeta for almost 40 years. She is married to Tommy Lee Jones and the mother of 4 wonderful kids and has 6 amazing grandchildren.

FAVORITE SCRIPTURE:
"For God so loved the world that he gave his one and only Son, that whoever believes in him shall not perish but have eternal life." John 3:16 NIV

NON-PROFIT ORGANIZATION:
LeaderShape

Learn more and DONATE here:
https://www.leadershape.org/

JJ's WHY: I have worked with this organization for over 15 years and I have witnessed young people's lives changed by participating.

CONNECT WITH JJ:

Facebook: Jennifer Jones
Instagram: jenniferjjjones33
LinkedIn: Jennifer (JJ) Jones
Email: jenniferjjjones33@gmail.com

TRACY D. VAULT, M.ED
Author, Educator, Mentor

 Tracy Vault is a native of Little Rock Arkansas. She now resides in the Atlanta, Georgia area since relocating in 2003. She completed her undergraduate program at Arkansas Baptist College in Little Rock, Arkansas with a Bachelors Degree in Human Services. After pondering and researching many graduate schools, it was decided that she would attend Argosy University for graduate school, she was accepted in 2004. Tracy received her Masters degree in Educational Leadership on May 10, 2006.

She strongly believes that God created all people with their own personal weaknesses and strengths. Through her experiences of working with a diverse population of people, she has grown to accept and respect the uniqueness of all people.

FAVORITE SCRIPTURE:
"Do not judge, or you too will be judged. For in the same way you judge others, you will be judged, and with the measure you use, it will be measured to you. Why do you look at the speck of sawdust in your brother's eye and pay no attention to the plank in your own eye?" Matthew 7:1-3 NIV

NON-PROFIT ORGANIZATION:
The Pink Tea Cup, Inc.

Learn more and DONATE here:
https://thepinkteacup.org/

TRACY'S WHY: The Pink Tea Cup, Inc. is a non-profit youth development for girls of color. The Pink Tea Cup Inc. is designed to develop girls of courage and compassion, while guiding girls through a self-awareness journey that inspires self-acceptance, self-love, self-trust, servitude, and the capacity to create worlds.

CONNECT WITH TRACY:

Facebook: Tracy Vault
Twitter: @traydai
Instagram: traydai
LinkedIn: Tracy Vault
Email: tdmckinney1989@gmail.com

DR. KELLY BULLOCK DAUGHERTY
Educator, Coach, National Trainer, Education Advocate/Consultant

Dr. Kelly Bullock Daugherty is a passionate educator who has worked in the urban school classroom setting for close to 20 years. In this capacity, she works not only as a classroom teacher, but a teacher leader and has represented her colleagues and school in several leadership roles. Additionally, Dr. Daugherty is an Education Advocate/Consultant for Transitions Educational Consulting, LLC, her personal business, where her scope of practice includes providing professional development in the areas of teacher efficacy, student engagement, and student motivation. Beyond that, she was previously a facilitator and member of the National Leadership Team for the Delta Teacher Efficacy Campaign in Washington, D.C.

She currently resides in Northeast Ohio with her husband, Leroy and their three children, Blair, Steven, and Kylee. In her spare time, Dr. Daugherty enjoys her role as an avid sports mom, spending time exercising, or having quiet time with family.

FAVORITE SCRIPTURE:

"Many are the plans in a person's heart, but it is the Lord's purpose that prevails." Proverbs 19:21 NIV

NON-PROFIT ORGANIZATION:
Virginia State University

Learn more and DONATE here:
http://www.vsu.edu/advancement/give-to-vsu.php

KELLY'S WHY: Virginia State is an HBCU close to my heart. It is my alma mater. I wanted to use this opportunity to support and advance the education of our young people. I thought it only fitting to give back to the land that set me on a course towards greatness!

CONNECT WITH DR. KELLY:

Facebook: Kelly Bullock Daugherty
Twitter: @DrKBDaugherty
Instagram: @DrKBDaugherty
LinkedIn: Dr. Kelly Bullock Daugherty
Email: TransitionsEducationalConsultant@gmail.com
Website:www.drkellydaugherty.com

TOWANDA WILSON
Author & Inspirational Speaker

It was an English assignment in the ninth grade that introduced Towanda Wilson to Maya Angelou's I Know Why The Caged Bird Sings. She was able to relate to Ms. Angelou on many levels and developed a sincere appreciation of her work. Towanda has always desired to be an Author due to her love for literature. She never fathomed using her own testimony nationally to inspire others until God showed her a vision many years ago. Though she attempted to run from what was shown to her, she later learned "If you want to make God laugh tell him YOUR plans for the life HE HAS ORDAINED FOR YOU!"

She continues to speak publicly and was acknowledged as a Blazing Star in 2018 by the Ann Arbor Club National Association of Negro Business Professional Women's Club, Inc. for "excellence in blazing the path forward and inspiring others to follow."

FAVORITE SCRIPTURE:

"Yet in all these things we are more than conquerors through Him who loved us." Romans 8:37 NKJV

NON-PROFIT ORGANIZATION:
Sickle Cell Disease Association of America, Michigan Chapter, Inc.

Learn more and DONATE here:
https://www.scdaami.org

TOWANDA'S WHY: Sickle Cell Disease affects one in every 1,000 babies that are born in the United States. More babies are diagnosed with Sickle Cell each year than cystic fibrosis or spina bifida and this disease affects people of all races and creeds. Sickle Cell Disease is a painful condition that affects everyone from babies to adults. I chose this organization because each donation allows us to work together in making a difference to "break the sickle cycle" by maximizing the quality of life of individuals living with the disease. Providing education and testing to the general public, and enabling individuals with the sickle cell trait to make informed decisions with respect to family planning decisions.

CONNECT WITH TOWANDA:

Facebook: www.facebook.com/towanda.wilsonwillis
Email: towandawilson46@gmail.com

TONI BROWN
Author & Educator

Toni Brown is a child of the King, wife, mother of two sons ages 13 and 11, and an advocate for children. Toni Brown has been an Educator of Literacy for 19+ years. She received her Educational Specialist Degree in AP Leadership and a Masters in Education from Nova Southeastern University. She also earned her Bachelors of Science degree from Bethune-Cookman University located in the beautiful Daytona, Beach Florida.

In 2011 God bestowed upon Toni the opportunity to reach one of her many goals and transition herself along with her children to a foreign country to educate students abroad. It was there that she began to embark on what her true calling is, inspiring and advocating for children.

FAVORITE SCRIPTURE:

"Have I not commanded you? Be strong and courageous. Do not be afraid; do not be discouraged, for the Lord your God will be with you wherever you go." Joshua 1:9 NIV

NON-PROFIT ORGANIZATION:
Alzheimer's Association

Learn more and DONATE here:
www.alz.org

TONI'S WHY: This disease has effected several of my loves ones and the results haven't been positive. I love the intensive research that has gone into finding a cure for this incurable brain disease.

CONNECT WITH TONI:
Facebook: Reading Cope
Instagram: trellgibson
Email: copeatl2016@gmail.com

NIKKI TIBBS
Author

A native Marylander, Nikki Tibbs is a Christian, a mother, and a working professional. She obtained a Bachelors of Science in Psychology with a Minor in Business Administration from UMUC at the age of 32, while working full time and raising a beautiful daughter. She has been blessed to work in many different fields from IT support, to Systems Testing, to Program Management.

She is currently a Master Scheduler with a Planning & Scheduling Professional (PSP) certification, supporting several vaccine and medical device programs for biodefense at a biopharmaceutical company. Nikki has been walking with the Lord since March 2006. While this is her first co-authoring of a book, she is excited to be able to add Co-Author to her list of accomplishments. Now, at the age of 43, she is an empty-nester and getting her second wind. She's excited to see how God will use her story to encourage others.

FAVORITE SCRIPTURE:

Be still, and know that I am God! Psalm 46:10 NIV

NON-PROFIT ORGANIZATION:
NAMI (National Alliance on Mental Health)

Learn more and DONATE here:
https://www.nami.org/

NIKKI'S WHY: I chose this organization because mental health issues are important to me. At the young age of 12, I was diagnosed with depression and was put on an anti-depressant. I overcame my bout with depression, but I have 2 family member who are currently in a fight with their mental health issues.

CONNECT WITH NIKKI:
Facebook: Nikki Tibbs
Twitter: @NIK_KNAK
Instagram: nix_blessed
LinkedIn: Nikki Tibbs
Email: ntibbs@yahoo.com

TEMEKA MILLER THOMAS, M.S.
Author & Inspirational Speaker

Temeka Miller Thomas was born and reared in Huntsville, Alabama and currently resides in her home state. She holds a Masters Degree in Human Relations and Management and is currently pursuing her licensed professional counselor (LPC) credentials. Professionally, she is honored to serve our nations heroes as a proud member of the advanced medical support team for the United States Department of Veteran Affairs.

With a heart of service and compassion for others, Temeka is happiest when she is sowing blessings into the lives of others. After suffering the traumatic loss of both her parents just seven months apart, Temeka is excited to share her story of faith in this work, alongside her talented co-authors. Temeka is the proud wife of Ricky Thomas, mother to Crimson and proud aunt to nieces and nephews, which she affectionately refers to her as "her heartbeats." (Jamison, Darreon, Dazell, Jaria, Makayla, Isabella and Raina.)

FAVORITE SCRIPTURE:

Though an army besiege me, my heart will not fear; though war break out against me, even then I will be confident." PSALM 27:13 NIV

NON-PROFIT ORGANIZATION:
The Journey Center in San Pedro De Macoris, Dominican Republic (DR)

Learn more and DONATE here:
journeytodestinyministries.org

TEMEKA'S WHY: I am an advocate for child welfare. I am a personal friend and supporter of the dynamic CEO and visionary, Ms. Felecia Y. Foster. She left her home in Memphis, TN in 2015 and moved to the DR to be a beacon of light for these children. I am amazed at the work that this organization is doing to rescue young girls in the Dominican Republic from human trafficking and various abusive situations.

CONNECT WITH TEMEKA:
Facebook: Temeka Miller
Twitter: @TemekaRenee2
Instagram: temekarenee74
Email: temekarenee@gmail.com

DURCUS HILLER
Educator and Author

Durcus Hiller is a Renaissance woman. She is committed to the clarion call and processes of becoming a stellar science and technology educator and facilitator. She believes that she is a valuable part of an august body of educators, fitted like pieces of a puzzle, unearthing, unveiling, and unfolding knowledge to impact the understanding and scruples of today's youth.

As a parent, education-advocate, and civic-minded member of society, she is an integral element of the learning community's success in preparing 21st century learners for the future. She believes that we live in a world of possibilities. She transfers that sentient as she fosters and cultivates a love for technology and science in her classroom.

FAVORITE SCRIPTURE:

Now this I know: The Lord gives victory to his anointed.

He answers him from his heavenly sanctuary with the victorious

power of his right hand. Psalm 20:6 NIV

NON-PROFIT ORGANIZATION:
National Multiple Sclerosis Foundation

Learn more and DONATE here:
https://www.nationalmssociety.org/

DURCUS' WHY: Extended family member has been afflicted by

the disease.

CONNECT WITH DURCUS:
Facebook: Roslynn Stewart
Twitter: @trawetszor
Instagram: just_scienze
Email: roslynnstewart@bellsouth.net

ULANDA ROCHELLE HUNTER
Author and Motivational Speaker

ULanda Rochelle Hunter is a proud mother of three children and two grandchildren. She currently works for a nonprofit organization that supports families by way of providing mental health resources and strategies to navigate children service systems. ULanda sees her work as her ministry.

Formerly a high school dropout, ULanda was able to beat all odds by furthering her education. On her journey she was able to secure a General Education Degree, Bachelors of Arts degree in Liberal Studies and lastly, a Master's of Science degree in Training & Development. In addition to her educational accomplishments, she is a certified Parent Peer Supporter.

She serves as a facilitator for parents and youth support groups through training and technical assistance. ULanda also serves as a Christian women's workshop coordinator and public speaker. Her spare time is filled with enjoying family, arts & crafts, traveling, being active in her community; with a primary focus on assisting youth and women. ULanda provides life and spiritual coaching to others, which inspired her to launch her own coaching business, "Next Level Coaching: You live it, Learn from it".

FAVORITE SCRIPTURE:
I can do all this through him who gives me strength. Philippians 4:13 NIV

NON-PROFIT ORGANIZATION:
Youth & Family Peer Support Alliance

Learn more and DONATE here:
www.ilalliance.org

ULANDA'S WHY: This organizational is designed to help support parents/families through difficult and challenging times. If helps to educate, inspire and provide hope through child serving systems in Illinois. Families who are trying to overcome obstacles due to a child/youth with Mental Health needs, that is effective all aspects of their lives. It helps to identity traumas and to help families to become more resilient.

CONNECT WITH ULANDA:
Facebook: ULanda Rochelle Hunter
Twitter: @ULandaHunter
Instagram: ulandahunter
Email: ulandarhunter@gmail.com

DR. NATALIE HOLTS DAVIS
Educator, Author, Motivational Speaker

Dr. Natalie Holts Davis is a caring, 20+ year veteran educator with a heart for God and passion for spreading the good news of Jesus! She is a savvy business professional, currently serving as a Coordinator of Federal Programs for the DeKalb County School District on the outskirts of metro Atlanta. She has been often recognized for her transparent, practical style of communicating and her engaging teaching ability.

Natalie is a wife and mom first. She has been married to her life's love, Demetrius Davis for 19 years and through this union, she has been blessed with four amazing children – Jasmine, Brittany, Cameron and Caleb. As a Georgia native, Natalie is the oldest of three children, born to the Rev. and Mrs. Nathaniel (Tonya) Holts. She holds a Bachelors degree in Business Administration from Augusta College, received her Middle Grades Teaching Certificate from Paine College (Augusta, GA), earned a Masters Degree in School Administration from Cambridge College (Boston, MA), and completed her studies at Argosy University Atlanta earning both a Specialist and Doctorate in Educational leadership. She is a faithful member of New Birth Missionary Baptist Church (Lithonia, GA) serving as a church leader on Usher Board #1 and with the Heart to Heart/Women on the Path ministry. Natalie enjoys traveling, eating good seafood, watching old movies, and serving the community as an active member of Delta Sigma Theta Sorority, Inc.

FAVORITE SCRIPTURE:
And we know that all things work together for good to those who love God, to those who are the called according to His purpose. Romans 8:28 NKJV

NON-PROFIT ORGANIZATION:
The National Multiple Sclerosis Society

Learn more and DONATE here:
https://www.nationalmssociety.org/

NATALIE'S WHY: My mother has lived with Multiple Sclerosis for over 35 years (most of her adult life). Seeing its crippling affects and knowing firsthand the debilitating grip that this disease has had on my mother and our entire family, I want to support finding a cure.

CONNECT WITH NATALIE:
Facebook: Natalie Davis **Twitter:** @DrNatalieDavis
LinkedIn: Natalie Davis, Ed.D.
Email: ndnextlevel@yahoo.com

CRYSTAL M. EDWARDS
Educator, Author, Speaker

In her professional life, Crystal M. Edwards is a school principal who uses research and evidence to support her ability to promote positive academic outcomes in her school. She is a staunch collaborator of staff, students and the community, to establish positive educational outcomes. When asked to speak on her role as a principal, she says, "I am a SERVANT of the PEOPLE! I wash the feet of the community!" Service to others remains her life's work, even in her private life.

Edwards is the visionary behind the innovative, non-profit organization, Empowering Single Moms, Inc. Edwards remains committed to the goal of self-sufficiency for single mothers to improve the lives of their children and future generations. Through financial, educational and emotional empowerment, she believes that the lives of single mothers can be transformed. She is a strategic and creative thinker poised to develop lasting solutions for the underserved. In her words, she is Pearson's wife and mother to the FANTASTIC 4: Aharon, Ahmani, Zebulon & Zion!

FAVORITE SCRIPTURE:
Instead of your shame you will receive a double portion, and instead of disgrace you will rejoice in your inheritance. And so you will inherit a double portion in your land, and everlasting joy will be yours. Isaiah 61:7 NIV

NON-PROFIT ORGANIZATION:
Empowering Single Moms, Inc.

Learn more and DONATE here:
www.empoweringsinglemomsinc.org

CRYSTAL'S WHY: I founded this non-profit. Empowering single Moms, Inc. is a 501(c)(3) committed to educating, housing and restoring single mothers receiving federal assistance by conducting self-sufficiency training, conflict resolution and educational programs.

CONNECT WITH CRYSTAL:
Facebook: CrystalSaidThat   **Twitter:** @CrystalSaidThat
Instagram: @CrystalSaidThat **LinkedIn:** Crystal M. Edwards
Email: President@EmpoweringSingleMomsInc.org
Website: www.empoweringsinglemomsinc.org

ELLE DEAN
Author, Educator, CEO Higher Levels Educational Group

Elle Dean is currently a Doctoral student at Texas A & M University at Commerce, with a prospective graduation date of May 2020. She earned both her Bachelors of Science and Masters of Education with a focus on Education Administration from the University of North Texas. During her 20+ year career she's worked as an elementary teacher, GED teacher, assistant principal, principal, bilingual specialist, elementary specialist, director, assistant superintendent and served interim Superintendent of DeSoto Independent School District.

Currently, Ms. Levels is the Assistant Superintendent for Student Support Services in DeSoto Independent School District. Owner of Higher Levels Educational Group, Ms. Levels has provided professional services to several school districts including Dallas, Garland, Austin, Tyler, Fort Worth, and several charter and private schools. She has several published research based articles. Ms. Levels is most proud of her role as mother to her children Leah and Lofton III.

FAVORITE SCRIPTURE:

"Whatsoever ye do, work heartily, as unto the Lord, and not unto men; knowing that the Lord ye shall receive the recompense of the inheritance: for ye serve the Lord Christ." Colossians 3:23-24 KJV

NON-PROFIT ORGANIZATION:
DeSoto ISD Education Foundation

Learn more and DONATE here:
http://www.desotoisd.org/departments/education_foundation

ELLE'S WHY: The primary focus of the Foundation is to provide funding for teachers to implement innovative experiences in the classroom and scholarships for graduating seniors.

CONNECT WITH ELLE:
Facebook: Levatta Levels
Twitter: @3lllevels
Instagram: treyelles
LinkedIn: Levatta Levels
Email: alllevels@yahoo.com

ALICIA D. FOUST
Author, Pastor, Educator

Alicia D. Foust is a North Carolina native. She is the mother of 3 handsome sons and one grandson. Alicia was educated in the Guilford and Person County school systems. She is an Author, educator and a pastor. She loves to empower the underdog. She firmly believes without change, growth is impossible.

FAVORITE SCRIPTURE:

"I consider that our present sufferings are not worth comparing with the glory that will be revealed in us." Romans 8:18 NIV

NON-PROFIT ORGANIZATION:
Delta Research and Educational Foundation

Learn more and DONATE here:
www.deltafoundation.net

ALICIA'S WHY: People perish for lack of knowledge. Education is extremely important. When people are informed they can make better decisions. People need to be taught.

Research helps us know the why and the how. Education and research are portals of wise investment because they hold the greatest residual affluence.

CONNECT WITH ALICIA:
Facebook: Alicia Foust
Twitter: @2ndRuach
Instagram: apostolicthunder
Email: apostle@ignitedblue.com
Website: www.ignitedblue.com

DR. CRYSTAL COOPER
Author, Speaker, Presenter

Crystal Cooper is an educator, school leader, and professional learning consultant. She majored in Elementary Education at William Paterson University and after obtaining a Masters and Specialists degree, she earned an Ed.D in Educational Leadership from the University of Georgia in 2018. Crystal believes in the power of prayer and sustaining faith through life's challenges. She utilizes writing to engage, inspire, and empower others to stand firm and live on purpose. Her relationship with God is most important to her as she builds strong relationships with family and friends. She enjoys working and supporting people from all walks of life. She is motivated in seeking opportunities to support the community and advocacy for all, especially children.

She currently resides in Georgia, and is now working on building an educational consultant agency as well as engaging in more published book opportunities.

FAVORITE SCRIPTURE:

"Trust in the Lord with all your heart and lean not on your own understanding; in all your ways submit to him, and he will make your paths straight." Proverbs 3:5-6 NIV

NON-PROFIT ORGANIZATION:
Delta Research and Educational Foundation;
Gwinnett County Chapter

Learn more and DONATE here:
www.deltafoundation.net

CRYSTAL'S WHY: This organization supports the community and students with scholarships and opportunities to enrich their lives, to attend colleges, to grow as leaders, and to grow academically. My affiliation as a member affords me the opportunity to contribute to their initiatives.

CONNECT WITH CRYSTAL:
Facebook: Crystal Cooper
Twitter: @drcooper74
Instagram: dr.cooper1913
LinkedIn: Dr. Crystal Cooper
Email: drcrystalcooper2018@gmail.com

YVONNE WILSON ANDERSON
Believer, Author, Financial Analyst,

Yvonne grew up in Washington, DC but relocated to Los Angeles, CA in the early nineties. She earned her undergraduate degree in Business Management and a graduate degree in Public Administration. She has experience working in finance as a budget analyst. She is also a believer, a sister, and auntie to eleven nieces and nephews.

FAVORITE SCRIPTURE:
"For with God nothing will be impossible." Luke 1:37 NKJV

NON-PROFIT ORGANIZATION:
NAASC-LA

Learn more and DONATE here:
naascla.org

YVONNE'S WHY: It is my alumni association.

CONNECT WITH YVONNE:
Facebook: Yvonne Wilson   Twitter: @Bunaire
Instagram: Bunaire   LinkedIn: Yvonne Wilson
Email: ywanderson@icloud.com

CRYSTAL C. CRUSE
Author & Virtual Assistant

Crystal Cruse was born July 3, 1981 to Patsy Bloom and the late Samuel Cruse. Crystal is the youngest of seven children and the mother of two beautiful and smart children; 16 year old son, and 8 year old daughter. Crystal works as a customer service adviser where her role entails a myriad of things; including but not limited to, supporting existing and potential customers; by providing helpful information, and answering questions about any service or product that she may be working with. Crystal also works with customers to de-escalate situations when they arise. She ensures that every customer that she speaks with or comes in contact with is completely satisfied with any and every question they may have had, and/or any product that they purchased.

She also serves as a Virtual Assistant for marketplace entrepreneurs, assisting them with scheduling, consistent communication, and building products for their customer base. Crystal's passions are cooking, working, and spending time with her family, extended family and friends. Crystal truly loves to worship and praise Yahweh mostly through music but she also enjoys a good word.

FAVORITE SCRIPTURE:

"…but the word of the Lord endures forever. And this is the word that was preached to you." 1 Peter 1:25 NIV

NON-PROFIT ORGANIZATION:
MOM-O

Learn more and DONATE here:
https://momocares.org/

CRYSTAL'S WHY: The primary focus of the Foundation is to provide funding for teachers to implement innovative experiences in the classroom and scholarships for graduating seniors.

CONNECT WITH CRYSTAL:
Facebook: Crystal Cruse
Instagram: humble2019
Email: cccruse@hearttoheartservices.com

ERICA M. DANIEL
Author, Speaker, Curator

Erica M. Daniel is a global health practitioner and citizen of the world. She is passionate about helping others identify their divine purpose. As a creative, she is the founder of Global Luminary Consulting, a travel curating firm and For the Love of Fufu, a Ghana based platform promoting interactive conversations and novel experiences. You can follow her on social media

FAVORITE SCRIPTURE:

"Brothers and sisters, I do not consider myself yet to have taken hold of it. But one thing I do: Forgetting what is behind and straining toward what is ahead, I press on toward the goal to win the prize for which God has called me heavenward in Christ Jesus." Philippians 3:13-14 NIV

NON-PROFIT ORGANIZATION:
Inspiring Minds

Learn more and DONATE here:
http://imyouth.org/

ERICA'S WHY: The primary focus of the foundation is to provide funding for teachers to implement innovative experiences in the classroom and scholarships for graduating seniors.

CONNECT WITH ERICA:
Facebook: @MsLuminary
Twitter: @MsLuminary
Instagram: msluminary
LinkedIn: @MsLuminary
Email: Daniel.ericam@gmail.com
Website: www.globalluminary.com

DANI KEYS
Author, CEO, Speaker

Danielle Vaughn moved to Fresno, California from Illinois where she completed her education in Communicative Sciences and Deaf Studies at Fresno State University where she also studied Business Management. Danielle is a single mother to three children with multiple disabilities. She is passionate about learning and helping both, parents of children with special needs, and those who live with the daily challenges of parenting children alone.

Danielle is the founder of Dani Keys also known as Keys 4 Needs where she manages the day-to-day operations of a non-profit organization which provides resources, support, and enrichment services for single moms and their children.

FAVORITE SCRIPTURE:

"She is more precious than rubies; nothing you desire can compare with her." Proverbs 3:15 NIV

NON-PROFIT ORGANIZATION
Community Keys 4 Needs Inc.

Learn more and DONATE here:
www.danikeys.org

DANI'S WHY: 81.4% of America is single mother households. There are so many programs that address children but not getting to the root of the problem which lies in the struggles of single mothers and we, as the Bible declares, want to honor from the head down not as the government from the feet up.

CONNECT WITH DANI:
Facebook: Community Keys 4 needs Inc.
Twitter: @KEYS4NEEDSINC
LinkedIn: Dani Keys
Email: dani@danikeys.org
Website:www.danikeys.org

ALMA R. ATKINSON
Author, Minister, & Entrepreneur

Alma R. Atkinson has been married for 34 years to Garry Atkinson. They have four adult children, a daughter-in-love, and a granddaughter. Alma is the fourth of six children, supported and reared by their father, grandparents, and aunt upon the death of their mother. Atkinson has used feelings of loss as fuel for encouragement and outreach. Her faith has sustained her through her journey of life.

Accepting Christ at an early age, and having a strong spiritual foundation, combined with a relationship with the Lord have allowed her to walk through adversity and experience victory in the face of opposition. Through forgiveness, true deliverance has now set her on a path of seeking God's best for her life. Having preached her initial sermon in 2015, Atkinson is a mentee of K.I.M. Mentoring Program and an entrepreneur.

FAVORITE SCRIPTURE:

"And the God of all grace, who called you to his eternal glory in Christ, after you have suffered a little while, will himself restore you and make you strong, firm and steadfast." I Peter 5:10 NIV

NON-PROFIT ORGANIZATION:
Raleigh Rescue Mission

Learn more and DONATE here:
https://www.raleighrescue.org/

ALMA'S WHY: Their New Life Plan, core values, mission, and focus on individuals and families.

CONNECT WITH ALMA:
Facebook: Alma Atkinson
Twitter: @AlmaRAtkinson1
Instagram: almaratkinson
Email: iamhopenow@gmail.com

MARVIN CRAIG
Author & Entrepreneur

Marvin Craig is a true man of faith, husband, and an amazing Father. Through a series of adversities as a child, Marvin rose to triumph by not becoming a statistic. Marvin has faced many traumas in his life, one major occurrence was finding his father dead at the prime age of 17, which spiraled him into additional life changing events. He is also a childhood survivor of cancer. Marvin has a pure heart and loves any and everything living unconditionally. He is always the first to apologize and forgive in most situations.

He is filled with a myriad of gifts and talents; he is very crafty with his hands inside and outside of the home. These gifts and passion have led him to a career of cement masonry and entrepreneurship. Many call him a "Jack of all trades" and consult him for guidance when trying to "fix" something from household projects and mechanic work to construction projects.

Marvin lives by the statement, "Don't ever say you can't do something," as this was what his father instilled in him as a little boy.

FAVORITE SCRIPTURE:

"Their loyalty is divided between God and the world, and they are unstable in everything they do." James 1:8 NLT

NON-PROFIT ORGANIZATION:
Delta Research and Educational Foundation

Learn more and DONATE here:
www.deltafoundation.net

MARVIN'S WHY: Education is a vital component of our journey. I have also witnessed my wife put countless hours into the educational initiatives at this organization.

CONNECT WITH MARVIN:
Facebook: Marvin Craig
Instagram: marvinstank.craig
Website: www.hearttoheartservices.com

PATSY CLOWNEY BLOOM
Author & Mentor

Patsy Clowney Bloom was born on December 25th and has always been a special Soul to all whom she was blessed to connect with along this journey. She is a wonderful wife, mother, sister, aunt, and friend. A nurturer by nature, Patsy has served as the caregiver to many throughout their life; even as they decline toward transition.

Patsy was raised in the church and has been a faithful member of the music and food ministries in her places of worship. Patsy spent her life working in textile mills, dry cleaners, fast food restaurants, and the NC Department of Corrections where she retired as a Corrections Officer. She has always been a person with an infectious sense of humor and a loves to dance. If you are feeling down or wrestling with life's problems; she is the person who can make you smile. Patsy has always been a "What you see is what you get" kind of person. She will always be her authentic self no matter where she is or who she is with.

FAVORITE SCRIPTURE:

"Look at the birds of the air; they do not sow or reap or store away in barns, and yet your heavenly Father feeds them. Are you not much more valuable than they?" Matthew 6:26 NIV

NON-PROFIT ORGANIZATION:
Delta Research and Educational Foundation

Learn more and DONATE here:
www.deltafoundation.net

PATSY'S WHY: The mission to create possibilities and improve lives for African American women and their families align to my personal mission.

CONNECT WITH PATSY:
Facebook: Patsy Clowney Bloom
Email: nloveafter60@yahoo.com

JA'QUEZ D. CRUSE
Author, Content Developer & Entrepreneur

Ja'Quez Cruse was raised by a fearless single mother who always emphasized education and a strong spiritual relationship with Abba Father. He is a perspective shifter, wordsmith, great thought partner, content developer for Heart 2 Heart Services, analytical thinker, and a connector for others in most all situations. Ja'Quez enjoys reading and writing poetry as well as thought provoking conversations. He graduated from DeKalb County School District and attended Albany State University after his high school graduation. The unthinkable Golden Ram experience was eye opening for him in many ways. He realized that this brief college experience was the beginning to the rest of his life. Ja'Quez learned many life lessons and transitioned back home. Blessed with twin girls, he had to make a more purposeful shift into parenthood and more importantly, manhood.

Ja'Quez has grown and is still growing standing on the principle that "the fear of the Lord is the beginning of wisdom." He is a published Author in the Heart 2 Heart Daily Devotional: A 31 Day Transformational Journey.

FAVORITE SCRIPTURE:

"Son of man, I have made you a watchman for the people of Israel; so hear the word I speak and give them warning from me. When I say to the wicked, 'You wicked person, you will surely die,' and you do not speak out to dissuade them from their ways, that wicked person will die for[a] their sin, and I will hold you accountable for their blood. But if you do warn the wicked person to turn from their ways and they do not do so, they will die for their sin, though you yourself will be saved." Ezekiel 33:7-9 NIV

NON-PROFIT ORGANIZATION:
Delta Research and Educational Foundation

Learn more and DONATE here:
www.deltafoundation.net

JA'QUEZ'S WHY: The mission to create possibilities and improve lives for African American women and their families align to my mission as women are an integral component to the family structure.

CONNECT WITH JA'QUEZ:
Facebook: Ja'Quez Cruse
Email: crusejaquez@yahoo.com

TEMIKA POWERS
Author & Minister

Minister Temika Powers, is the wife of Pastor Lorenzo Powers, they are blessed with four wonderful children; Kamaya, Anthony, Malcolm and Lauryn. She is the Elect Lady of Kingdom Keys United, in Piedmont SC. Minister Temika Powers became a licensed Minister of the gospel in May 2003, and previously served as a youth pastor and Minister of Music. She is a true woman of God, devoting her life to the purpose in which God has predestined for her. She has a kind and open spirit that reaches out to everyone she comes in contact with, her loving spirit sets her apart from others. She loves to assist others, loves to see people smile, and lives by the motto "If you change the way you think, you will change the way you live."

Minister Temika is currently pursuing a degree in Science and Criminal Justice at Brown Mackie College. Her plans are to become a Social Worker in order to counsel children and families. Minister Temika strives to be an example of a virtuous woman — a woman who is yielded to God in every area of her life. The Lord has given her a passion for people and Minister Temika continues to aim toward and produce excellence in each ministry opportunity God allots to her.

FAVORITE SCRIPTURE:

"Lift up your heads, you gates; be lifted up, you ancient doors that the King of glory may come in. Who is this King of glory? The Lord strong and mighty, the Lord mighty in battle. Lift up your heads, you gates; lift them up, you ancient doors, that the King of glory may come in. Who is he, this King of glory? The Lord Almighty— he is the King of glory." Psalm 24:7-10 NIV

NON-PROFIT ORGANIZATION:
Kingdom Keys United

Learn more and DONATE here:
Facebook: Kingdom Keys United

TEMIKA'S WHY: This ministry was birthed out of obedience and entrusted to my husband and I. All donations are welcomed to increase the Kingdom impact.

CONNECT WITH TEMIKA:
Facebook: Kingdom Keys United
Email: kingdomkeysunited@gmail.com

KENYA C. POSEY
Author, Nurse, Realtor & Credit Consultant

Kenya Currie Posey was born in Kannapolis, NC she is a graduate from A.L. Brown High School, class of 1993. She studied at NC State University and graduated from UNC-Charlotte in 1999, with a Psychology/Sociology degree. She went on to obtain an Associates Degree in Nursing from Guilford Technical Community College. Kenya is married and has two children.

She currently resides in Las Vegas, NV with her husband and daughter where she works fulltime as a Registered Nurse, licensed Realtor, and Credit Consultant. Kenya enjoys networking and meeting new people. Kenya also enjoys traveling with her friends and family exploring different parts of the world. She has a passion for helping others, teaching, and training. Kenya looks forward to growing her real estate business in order to leave a legacy for her children.

FAVORITE SCRIPTURE:

"For the Spirit God gave us does not make us timid, but gives us power, love and self-discipline." 2 Timothy 1:7 NIV

NON-PROFIT ORGANIZATION:
National Black Child Development Institute

Learn more and DONATE here:
https://www.nbcdi.org/

KENYA'S WHY: My sister, Dr. Ashelin Currie works with this organization within the Detroit community allowing African American children to have access to books, reading, and creative learning that they are not exposed to in their community. I aim to support this project so that our youth are provided a supportive environment to build their reading skills.

CONNECT WITH KENYA:
Facebook: Kenya Posey – Realtor #KWSouthernNevada
Twitter: @kposeyrealtor
Instagram: kenyaposeyrealtor
LinkedIn: Kenya Posey
Email: refineimagellc@gmail.com
Website:https://kposey.kw.com/

DR. J. LE'RAY

Author, Life Coach, Educator, Strategist & Thought Partner

Dr. Johni Le'Ray Cruse Craig is a spirit on a journey serving in many capacities to complete her divine assignments as she walks boldly and confidently in her divine calling as a Shifter, Connector, and Exhorter. As the Founder/CEO/Creative Visionary for Heart to Heart Services, LLC., Dr. J. Le'Ray connects with her clients Heart 2 Heart to provide a myriad of services as a three time bestselling Published Author, Speaker, Workshop Facilitator, Event Planner, Caterer, Life Coach & Visionary Curator of published works with distinct purposes. She is passionate about HEART matters and knows that everything is rooted from the heart.

She is an Educator and serves as an education advocate through leading professional development workshops, seminars and institutes. Her patented belief, "Education: It's A Heart Matter®" is her foundational truth and is the focus of her divine assignments; in shifting others to understand that everyone is an educator and teaching from the heart is most effective and impactful. Additionally, her heart is committed to shifting souls' mindsets and perspectives through mentoring and life coaching.

She has published four books; *Heart 2 Heart Daily Devotional: 31 Day Transformational Journey* and The *Transforming the S.A.W (Spots And Wrinkles)* Journal, *Still Have Joy* Anthology, *It Take Money Honey* Anthology, two notebooks and a digital anthology, *Found in Favor*, written and published several scholarly journals and op-ed articles. She has built a Rise Holy Spirit Rise Masterclass, created topical curriculum and courses around several spiritual matters in life coaching series and other masterclasses.

FAVORITE SCRIPTURE:

"And we know that in all things God works for the good of those who love him, who have been called according to his purpose."
Romans 8:28 NIV

NON-PROFIT ORGANIZATION
Delta Research & Educational Foundation

Learn more and DONATE here:
www.deltafoundation.net

DR J. LE'RAY'S WHY: Education: It's A Heart Matter®

CONNECT WITH DR. J. LE'RAY:
Facebook: Author Dr. J. Le'Ray   Twitter: @1PositiveSpirit
Instagram: drjleray.heartcoach
LinkedIn: Dr. J. Le'Ray Cruse Craig
Email: drjleray@hearttoheartservices.com
Website: www.hearttoheartservices.com

VERGANELL THOMAS CRAIG
Author, Evangelist & Missionary

Evangelist Verganell Craig is from the state of Mississippi where she is a Homemaker and a retiree; after over 14 years as a Family Protection Specialist with Child Protective Services. Verganell is presently a Foster Parent for the state of Mississippi. She is a member of Paradise Church of God in Christ in Meridian, under the leadership of pastor Elder Alfonso and First Lady Vanessa Wilson, where she servers as Evangelist Missionary. She is very active in the local and district women's ministry. She is a lover of God and people. Verganell has received numerous certifications for her community services concerning families for providing safety, and healthy living environments.

Verganell received her high school diploma in 1972, from Choctaw County High School in Butler, Alabama; an Associates Degree, 2005 from Meridian Community College, Meridian, Mississippi and her Bachelors of Science in Social Work, 2007 from Mississippi State University. She is the mother of four biological children, 13 grands, and 8 great grands and about 10-15 foster children have lived in her home.

FAVORITE SCRIPTURE:

"Therefore, as we have opportunity, let us do good to all people, especially to those who belong to the family of believers." Galatians 6:10 NIV

NON-PROFIT ORGANIZATION:
Ora Lee Smith Cancer Research Foundation

Learn more and DONATE here:
https://weareoralee.org/

VERGANELLS'S WHY: I have lost several family members and friends to cancer and I pray that a cure can be found.

CONNECT WITH VERGANELL:
Email:Nellthomas64@gmail.com

Additional Literary
Works Available
By: Dr. J. Le'Ray

www.hearttoheartservices.com

Book	**Book**	**Anthology Book**
http://bit.ly/H2HDD	http://bit.ly/TTSAW	http://bit.ly/JCCStillHaveJoy

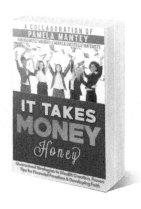

Anthology Book	**Digital Anthology**	**Notebook**
http://bit.ly/ITMHJCC	http://bit.ly/FIFAnthol	http://bit.ly/RHRNotebook

62046931R00157

Made in the USA
Columbia, SC
29 June 2019